Scrapbooking Your
Family History
❧ THE ULTIMATE WORKBOOK ❧

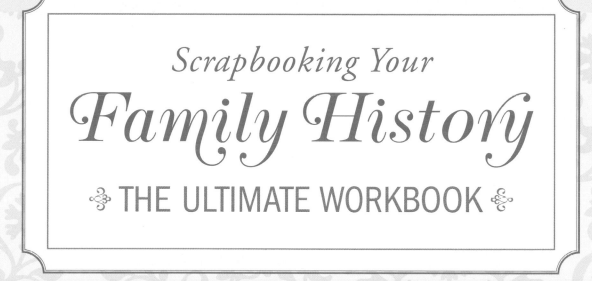

A guided plan for organizing and telling your family stories

A LEISURE ARTS PUBLICATION

LEISURE ARTS
the art of everyday living

Vice President and Editor-in-Chief   SANDRA GRAHAM CASE

Executive Director of Publications   CHERYL NODINE GUNNELLS

Senior Publications Director   SUSAN WHITE SULLIVAN

Special Projects Director   SUSAN FRANTZ WILES

Director of Designer Relations   DEBRA NETTLES

Senior Prepress Director   MARK HAWKINS

Publishing Systems Administrator   BECKY RIDDLE

Publishing Systems Assistants   CLINT HANSON, JOHN ROSE, and KEIJI YUMOTO

Vice President and Chief Operating Officer   TOM SIEBENMORGEN

Director of Corporate Planning and Development   LATICIA MULL DITTRICH

Vice President, Sales and Marketing   PAM STEBBINS

Director of Sales and Services   MARGARET REINOLD

Vice President, Operations   JIM DITTRICH

Comptroller, Operations   ROB THIEME

Retail Customer Service Manager   STAN RAYNOR

Print Production Manager   FRED F. PRUSS

Publisher Information

Copyright © 2007 Leisure Arts, Inc.

5701 Ranch Drive, Little Rock, Arkansas 72223-9633

Editor-In-Chief   TRACY WHITE

Senior Writer   RACHEL THOMAE

Associate Editor   MAURIANNE DUNN

Contributing Writer   HEATHER JONES

Copy Editor   KIM SANDOVAL

Editorial Assistants   JOANNIE McBRIDE,
FRED BREWER, LIESL RUSSELL

Creative Director   BRIAN TIPPETTS

Art Director, Special Projects   ERIN BAYLESS

Illustrator   ANNALISE NEIL

CK MEDIA

Chief Executive Officer   DAVID O'NEIL

Creative Director/Founder   LISA BEARNSON

Chief Financial Officer/Chief Operating Officer   RICH FANKHAUSER

VP/Consumer Marketing Director   SUSAN DuBOIS

Director of Events   PAULA KRAEMER

Group Publisher/Quilting   TINA BATTOCK

White, Tracy
Creating Keepsakes
"A Leisure Arts Publication"

ISBN-**13**: 978-**1**-60140-528-9
ISBN-**10**: 1-60140-528-6

Family Stories,
LOST AND FOUND

GROWING UP, I THOUGHT I WAS THE RICHEST GIRL IN THE WORLD. We had a big two-story house, took a fun vacation to my grandma's farm in Missouri every summer and always got to eat out on our birthdays. We spent uninterrupted time together as a family every Monday night, and on Sunday evenings, my mom would make waffles, and we'd all play games together.

Looking back on my childhood, I wish I had a scrapbook to remember all the wonderful moments we spent together. Unfortunately, Mom didn't keep a scrapbook of my childhood, and in fact, I only have two photographs of myself as a baby—and one very sparse baby book (see opposite page) that my mom tried to write in during my first few years. It's sad how this baby book is literally crumbling before my eyes, due to acidic paper and the wrong type of adhesive.

As my parents grow older, I realize that now is the time to find out more about my childhood and to record those special moments that I never want to forget. This workbook helped me get started on that process—I just turned to the worksheet pages in the baby chapter, selected a few questions and interviewed my mom. I printed out her answers and placed them right on my scrapbook page. I love the quick and easy results, and I'm happy that my baby photographs are now safely preserved for my future generations to enjoy.

Ready to start your family history projects? This workbook is a wonderful starting place, full of checklists, forms, page planners, worksheets, scrapbook-page ideas and more. Enjoy discovering and sharing your favorite family stories!

Lisa Bearnson

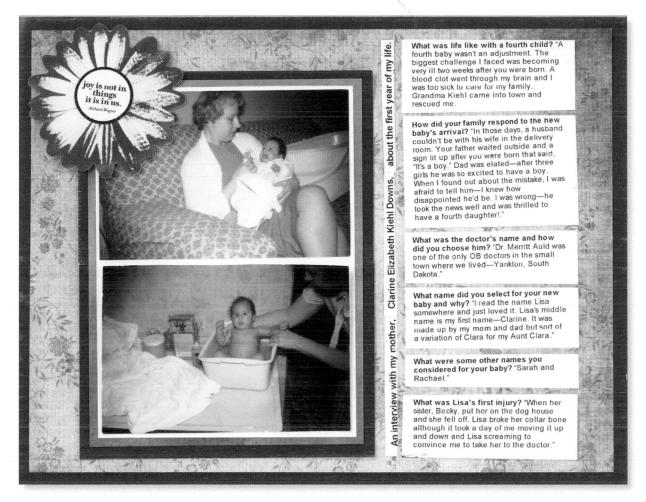

An interview with my mother, Clarine Elizabeth Kiehl Downs, about the first year of my life.

What was life like with a fourth child? "A fourth baby wasn't an adjustment. The biggest challenge I faced was becoming very ill two weeks after you were born. A blood clot went through my brain and I was too sick to care for my family. Grandma Kiehl came into town and rescued me.

How did your family respond to the new baby's arrival? "In those days, a husband couldn't be with his wife in the delivery room. Your father waited outside and a sign lit up after you were born that said, "It's a boy." Dad was elated—after three girls he was so excited to have a boy. When I found out about the mistake, I was afraid to tell him—I knew how disappointed he'd be. I was wrong—he took the news well and was thrilled to have a fourth daughter!."

What was the doctor's name and how did you choose him? "Dr. Merritt Auld was one of the only OB doctors in the small town where we lived—Yankton, South Dakota."

What name did you select for your new baby and why? "I read the name Lisa somewhere and just loved it. Lisa's middle name is my first name—Clarine. It was made up by my mom and dad but sort of a variation of Clara for my Aunt Clara."

What were some other names you considered for your baby? "Sarah and Rachael."

What was Lisa's first injury? "When her sister, Becky, put her on the dog house and she fell off. Lisa broke her collar bone although it took a day of me moving it up and down and Lisa screaming to convince me to take her to the doctor."

joy is not in things it is in us.
—Richard Wagner

An Interview with My Mother BY LISA BEARNSON

Contents

Bonus

See page 11 to learn how to download all of the checklists, forms, page planners and worksheets in this book for FREE.

Introduction

YOU'VE JUST INHERITED BOXES OF FAMILY PHOTOS FROM A family member, and you're fascinated by the snapshots and memorabilia. So many memories! And, perhaps, so little time to sort them out. You may be feeling a bit overwhelmed. And you probably have lots of questions, ranging from, "How can I put these photographs in order?" to "How can I best find and tell our family stories?"

At first, it may seem like you have more questions than answers. As you look through the photographs in each box, you find snapshots of your parents as young children and realize you didn't know your mom played softball. You find photographs of your grandparents as a young couple and wonder if they met at school or at church, or maybe at a dance. You find photographs of your great-great-grandparents and muse about what life was like for them on the day they were photographed, so solemn and formal in their wedding attire.

Perhaps some of the photographs have names and dates, but some of them don't. There are church programs, sales brochures, faded receipts, business cards, a group of letters tied with a velvet ribbon and more. You know these boxes are full of stories waiting to be told—but which stories do you tell? And how?

This workbook will help you find the answers to your questions and will help you get your family history started (and keep it going!). Enjoy the process of learning more about your family—and maybe even a little more about yourself!

HOW TO GET STARTED

Ready to get started scrapbooking your family history? Take it one step at a time, and you'll be on your way before you know it! Here's an easy way to begin.

1. Read the "Getting Started" chapter. Choose the type of project you want to create and start gathering information and photographs to complete your scrapbook pages.

2. Read through the chapters and make a list of the family stories you want to tell. Photocopy or download the ready-to-use checklists and worksheets in each chapter and begin to fill in the information. See the link below for download information.

3. Slip completed worksheets into sheer protectors and store them in a three-ring binder, or use the worksheets as starting points for creating your own scrapbook pages. The page planners at the end of each chapter will help you decide where to place your journaling, page titles and photographs.

Bonus: FREE DOWNLOADS

All of the checklists, templates and worksheets in this book can be downloaded for free. These ready-to-use forms can be printed as many times as you'd like and can be filled in, cut out or used however you choose.

Downloads include:

❖ *Checklists.* Use the checklists to organize your projects, to make decisions about what stories you want to tell and to start gathering information.

❖ *Forms.* Want to add a family tree to your layout or looking for an easy way to record family information? The helpful forms in this book can be downloaded at full-size from the websites listed below.

❖ *Page Planners.* Need a simple plan to follow for creating your own scrapbook pages? Use the page planners at the end of each chapter as starting points for your own layouts. Or print them onto cardstock and add your own photographs, words and journaling directly onto the pages.

❖ *Worksheets.* Our interview-style worksheets will help you gather and record information on a variety of favorite family topics.

Download forms for free from:

Creating Keepsakes, *www.creatingkeepsakes.com/familyhistoryworkbook*
Leisure Arts, *www.leisurearts.com/familyhistory*

chapter 1

Getting Started

"The secret of getting ahead is getting started."
— *Mark Twain*

Choose a project.

S

antonia & anton

Anton Kovac (my dad's paternal grandpa) was born to Ann & Louis Kovac on June 8, 1865 in Lubilanja, Yugoslavia. Antonia Kovac (my dad's paternal grandma…and, yes, her maiden name was Kovac…apparently the two were cousins though no one is clear on how close the relation was) was born to Primus & Frances Kovac on January 17, 1875 in Preserje, Yugoslavia. Both families came to the United States and settled initially in Montana, where Anton changed his last name to Smith in efforts to become more "American"…apparently "Kovac" means "blacksmith" in Slovanian. The couple was the first to be married by Rev. John Piqnat in Anaconda, MT on June 11, 1896. They had fourteen children, all born in East Helena, MT. The family moved to Prosser, WA in 1918 where they lived to celebrate their 50th anniversary in 1946. Anton died on March 17, 1950 in Prosser (at almost 85 years old) and Antonia followed shortly thereafter on April 28, 1950 at the age of 75.

1946 anniversary photos. TOP: Antonia & Anton. BOTTOM: (back) Frank, Anthony, Rudolph (Buck), Stephen, Jack (John), Ignatius…(front) Mary Smith Maver, Antonia Smith (mother), Anton Smith (father), Emma Smith Novak.

Antonia & Anton BY AMANDA PROBST

Tip: As I was gathering pictures and trying to sort out how I wanted to approach the huge undertaking of documenting my family history, I discovered that what I truly wanted to capture was the relationships over the years. In particular, I wanted to cover ancestors as individuals, as siblings, as couples and as parents.

—Amanda Probst

Checklist

PROJECT TYPES

You can take so many different approaches to scrapbooking your family history! Choose the one that feels best to you. Remember, there's no right or wrong way to save your family stories, and your "history" can be just a few pages or an entire album. Here are some possible topics to help you choose the perfect project for you:

- All About Me

- Complete Family History

- Family Recipes

- Family Stories

- Family Traditions

- Favorite Childhood Memories

- Lessons I've Learned from Mother/Father

- Marriage: The First Year and Other Important Milestones

- My Memories of . . . (enter a person's name)

- School Memories

- Tribute to a Loved One

- Year in Review

THE BABY OF THE FAMILY

According to his big sisters, your Papa Robert made an adorable priest when the Smith kids would "play" church. As the youngest of eight, Papa Robert likely didn't have much say in the matter. Still, he says he had a great childhood and got along well with all of his brothers and sisters, though, of course, his big brother Jim would sometimes pick on him as good big brothers do. (His sisters say that Papa Robert was a quiet and perfect child, small for his age, "fragile" and definitely the introvert of the twins.) Papa Robert says that the youngest four, Barb, Jim and the twins, he and Rose, were particularly close. Growing up, he has fond memories of games on Sundays, especially baseball with "Smith rules" including chicken house homeruns and ricochets off the grain elevator. They all also enjoyed board games like Monopoly, though not all at the same time. When asked what sort of chores he was responsible for, my dad says that his big sister Cathy would answer that the boys didn't do anything. Papa Robert, though, remembers tasks like clearing the table, dusting, weeding the garden, mowing and helping with outside farm work. Knowing my dad and having seen him and his siblings all together, I can believe that he truly did get along well with all of them and am frankly amazed.

The Baby of the Family BY AMANDA PROBST

Tip: I've been scanning all of the family photos that have come my way and organizing them into computer folders according to family. For each photo, I name the file according to the year and the people pictured. If more information is available, I have a companion text document where I type the name of the photo image and then add whatever information I have. —*Amanda Probst*

Checklist

PROJECT ORGANIZATION

How do you organize your photographs and memorabilia? This checklist will help you choose the best organization method for you.

DIGITAL PHOTOS

- ☐ Organize scanned or digital photos with photo-organization software.

- ☐ Burn images onto CDs for safekeeping.

- ☐ Start an online photo album to share photos with family and friends.

PRINTED PHOTOS

- ☐ Organize photos chronologically, by subject or by each individual in your family in archival photo boxes, photo storage cases or totes. Use divider tabs, envelopes or index cards for each section.

- ☐ Display family photos in collage frames.

- ☐ Slide photos into albums with photo sleeves. (Remember never to use magnetic albums.)

- ☐ Don't forget about the memories that are being created right now! Keep one or two plastic containers on hand to store all of your memorabilia.

PRINTED AND DIGITAL PHOTOS

- ☐ Consider hiring someone to do the work for you. There are many reputable companies who have made it their business to help organize and document memorabilia, photos and digital files.

A few notes:

- ❧ Whatever your organization method, be sure to store photos away from light and moisture, and avoid areas that run the risk of water damage.

- ❧ Be sure to label each picture so future generations will have the information to go along with the priceless images. Use a soft graphite pencil, fine-point marker or permanent pen that is waterproof, odorless and permanent. Never use a ballpoint pen.

Make time for family history.

When this you see, remember me . . .

It was Marian's idea to have this photo taken right before my Grandfather, Art went off to war. She insisted all three sisters wear black blouses and pearls. It's such a beautiful portrait and extra special since the three of them never got together again for studio photo. Marian has since passed on from breast cancer. But, thanks to her, we will always remember this special time. Left to right: Esther (Grandmother), Martha and Marian Koivisto

1943

When This You See BY KIM KESTI

Tip: Save time by keeping your design simple. I completed this page in less than an hour! —*Kim Kesti*

Checklist

FINDING TIME

Starting on your family history can feel overwhelming. But if you break your project down into manageable pieces, you'll find you can accomplish much more than you ever would have imagined!

Here's a checklist of family history scrapbooking activities you can complete in less than an hour. Think of family history as a series of steps—it's perfectly fine to take one step at a time!

☐ Write down the answers to a few questions in this workbook.

☐ Organize a packet or two of photographs.

☐ Scan and print an old photograph.

☐ Send a short e-mail to a family member requesting information.

☐ Call a family member and ask him or her to share memories about a life event.

☐ Journal about a family member (type the journaling on your computer and print it).

☐ Visit a family history website and research your family.

☐ Choose cardstock, patterned papers and embellishments for a scrapbook page.

☐ Create a pretty scrapbook page (use the page planners in this book to help you get started).

Plan a one-photo layout.

Family Portrait 1943

This is my favorite photo of Dad's family. I love the combination of carefully chosen outfits and those crumpled socks and scuffed shoes. I imagine this portrait sitting was quite a splurge for my Grandparents; they weren't very well off. Sitting from left to right: Lora Jeanne, Lyle Edwin (Dad) and Wayne Lee Smith.

Family Portrait BY KIM KESTI

Tip: When I want to create a layout in a short amount of time, I start by printing my journaling on plain cardstock. I trim it later so I don't have to worry about lining anything up. For this page, I also chose two coordinating papers and created a simple, quick accent by mimicking the flower in the patterned paper.

—Kim Kesti

Checklist

ONE-PHOTO LAYOUT PLANNER

To plan a one-photo page, choose from the following options:

1. I will place my photo:
   - ☐ In the middle of the page.
   - ☐ In the bottom-left corner of the page.
   - ☐ In the upper half of the page.

2. To tell my story, I need at least a:
   - ☐ 4" x 4" square photo.
   - ☐ 4" x 6" rectangle photo.
   - ☐ 6" x 6" square photo.

3. To add interest to the page I will:
   - ☐ Cluster a few buttons in one corner.
   - ☐ Add a few strips of ribbon.
   - ☐ Use a rub-on or sticker phrase.

4. What do I want my family to know about this photo?

....

....

....

....

5. What unexpected detail or personal insight can I include in my journaling to add a unique twist?

....

....

....

Plan a two-photo layout.

I would love to know more about these photos of my great grandfather and grandfather. Garrett and James Sullivan. We know they were taken at the general store. And it's obvious to me that my grandfather was emulating his dad. I love that! Circa 1924

Father and Son BY SHELLEY LAMING

Checklist

TWO-PHOTO LAYOUT PLANNER

To plan a two-photo page, choose from the following options:

1. My photos will be:
   - ☐ Both 4" x 6" or both 3" x 5".
   - ☐ One 4" x 6" and one 3" x 5".
   - ☐ Cropped.

2. I will place my photos:
   - ☐ Overlapping one another.
   - ☐ Separate from each other but grouped in the same area.
   - ☐ In different areas of the page.

3. For my journaling I will:
   - ☐ Include basic factual information beneath each photo.
   - ☐ Use a journaling block and include information about both photos in paragraph form.
   - ☐ Include quotes and fond memories about the person shown in the photograph.

4. When I look at this layout 10 years from now, what will I wish I had included that I'm not planning to include?

   ....

   ....

5. In regard to paper selection, what colors or patterns will portray the emotion about this event or paint a picture about this individual's personality?

   ....

   ....

Nita Kay

I cherish these portraits taken of my mom when she was about five years old. Fine photography was a luxury they couldn't afford very often. Grandma traded sewing for portraits taken by a neighborhood friend.

Nita Kay BY SHELLEY LAMING

Checklist

WHAT SUPPLIES WILL I NEED?

Before you start scrapbooking, it's helpful to gather some basic supplies. You'll want to make sure your materials are archival quality so your finished project will last for several generations. Look for words like "archival" or "photo safe" on product packaging.

For a basic page, start with supplies like:

- ☐ Cardstock
- ☐ Photo corners and/or adhesive
- ☐ A pen (for journaling)
- ☐ A paper trimmer or pair of scissors

For an embellished page, add supplies like:

- ☐ Ribbon
- ☐ Flowers
- ☐ Stickers or rub-ons
- ☐ Charms
- ☐ Buttons

You can store your completed pages in sheet protectors and then keep the finished pages in:

- ☐ A scrapbook album (Check your local craft, discount and scrapbook stores for options.)
- ☐ A basic binder (Check your office supply store for options.)

Find information about your family.

a new life

Ida Svenson was born on September 17, 1859 in Jönköping, Småland, Sweden. Per Albert Julin was born on January 15, 1853 in Kristinehamm, Värmland, Sweden. These two people were my great, great grandparents. They immigrated to the United States with their families. They were married on December 1, 1877 in Chicago, Illinois. This is their wedding photo. My great grandmother, Minnie Ida, was born to them in Chicago in 1878. They lived in Chicago until August 13, 1894 when the family purchased an 80 acre farm in Maiden Rock, Wisconsin and moved there. Minnie met and married Lewis D. Trumbull in Maiden Rock, a town that Lewis' father, John D. Trumbull, had founded. My grandmother Lucile was born in Maiden Rock in 1904. Per passed away September 14, 1911. Ida lived another 32 years without him. She passed away on August 4, 1943.

-Information from the Wisconsin State Genealogical Society

Per and Ida Julin
December 1, 1877

A New Life BY VICKI HARVEY

Tip: Many states have genealogical societies that are brimming with information. My great-uncle gathered most of this information from the Wisconsin State Genealogical Society. —*Vicki Harvey*

Checklist

PLACES TO FIND INFORMATION

Want to know more about the photographs in your possession? Start with your family members and then hunt for journals; scrapbooks; old letters; family Bibles; copies of birth, marriage and death certificates; photographs; school records; military records; obituaries; deeds and wills. You may be able to find these kinds of documents in the following locations:

- ☐ Family history libraries

- ☐ The local library in the town where your family lived

- ☐ Old newspaper articles

- ☐ School yearbooks

- ☐ The Internet (see links on page 29)

- ☐ Courthouses

- ☐ Churches

- ☐ Government offices
  Note: Be sure to check all jurisdictions (town, county, state and country).

- ☐ Historical societies

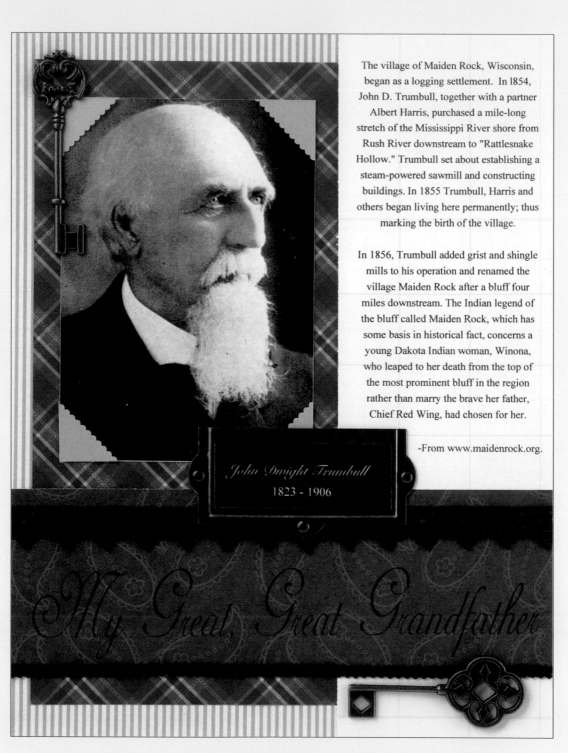

The village of Maiden Rock, Wisconsin, began as a logging settlement. In 1854, John D. Trumbull, together with a partner Albert Harris, purchased a mile-long stretch of the Mississippi River shore from Rush River downstream to "Rattlesnake Hollow." Trumbull set about establishing a steam-powered sawmill and constructing buildings. In 1855 Trumbull, Harris and others began living here permanently; thus marking the birth of the village.

In 1856, Trumbull added grist and shingle mills to his operation and renamed the village Maiden Rock after a bluff four miles downstream. The Indian legend of the bluff called Maiden Rock, which has some basis in historical fact, concerns a young Dakota Indian woman, Winona, who leaped to her death from the top of the most prominent bluff in the region rather than marry the brave her father, Chief Red Wing, had chosen for her.

-From www.maidenrock.org.

John Dwight Trumbull
1823 - 1906

My Great Great Grandfather

My Great-Great-Grandfather BY VICKI HARVEY

Tip: Look on the Internet for family history information. Search a variety of sites, like the website of the town where your ancestors lived. —*Vicki Harvey*

Checklist

FAMILY HISTORY INTERNET SITES

- Ancestry.com (*www.ancestry.com*)

- BYU Family History Library (*www.lib.byu.edu/fslab/*)

- Cyndi's List (*www.cyndislist.com*)

- Family Search (*www.familysearch.org*)

- Genealogical Database Network (*www.geneanet.org*)

- Genealogy.com (*www.genealogy.com*)

- Helm's Genealogy Toolbox (*www.onlinegenealogy.com*)

- Kindred Konnections (*www.kindredkonnections.com*)

- Library of Congress (*www.loc.gov*)

- The National Archives and Records Administration (*www.nara.gov*)

- North American Genealogy Resources (*www.genhomepage.com/northamerican.html*)

- Online Genealogical Database Index (*www.gentree.com*)

- Roots Web Genealogical Data Cooperative (*www.rootsweb.com*)

- Surname Web (*www.surnameweb.org*)

- U.S. Census Bureau (*www.census.gov*)

- U.S. GenWeb Project (*www.usgenweb.com*)

- World GenWeb Project (*www.worldgenweb.org*)

If you're looking for living relatives, try these sites:

- Four11: The Internet White Pages (*www.four11.com*)

- Switchboard: The People and Business Directory (*www.switchboard.com*)

- The Ultimate Directory (*www.infospace.com*)

Request help from family members.

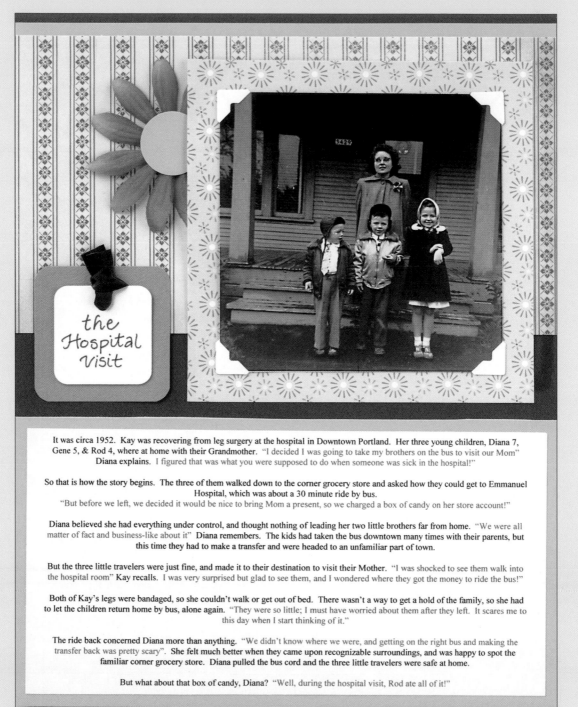

It was circa 1952. Kay was recovering from leg surgery at the hospital in Downtown Portland. Her three young children, Diana 7, Gene 5, & Rod 4, where at home with their Grandmother. "I decided I was going to take my brothers on the bus to visit our Mom" Diana explains. I figured that was what you were supposed to do when someone was sick in the hospital!"

So that is how the story begins. The three of them walked down to the corner grocery store and asked how they could get to Emmanuel Hospital, which was about a 30 minute ride by bus.
"But before we left, we decided it would be nice to bring Mom a present, so we charged a box of candy on her store account!"

Diana believed she had everything under control, and thought nothing of leading her two little brothers far from home. "We were all matter of fact and business-like about it" Diana remembers. The kids had taken the bus downtown many times with their parents, but this time they had to make a transfer and were headed to an unfamiliar part of town.

But the three little travelers were just fine, and made it to their destination to visit their Mother. "I was shocked to see them walk into the hospital room" Kay recalls. I was very surprised but glad to see them, and I wondered where they got the money to ride the bus!"

Both of Kay's legs were bandaged, so she couldn't walk or get out of bed. There wasn't a way to get a hold of the family, so she had to let the children return home by bus, alone again. "They were so little; I must have worried about them after they left. It scares me to this day when I start thinking of it."

The ride back concerned Diana more than anything. "We didn't know where we were, and getting on the right bus and making the transfer back was pretty scary". She felt much better when they came upon recognizable surroundings, and was happy to spot the familiar corner grocery store. Diana pulled the bus cord and the three little travelers were safe at home.

But what about that box of candy, Diana? "Well, during the hospital visit, Rod ate all of it!"

The Hospital Visit BY LEAH LaMONTAGNE

Tip: When your journaling includes comments or quotes from multiple people, make it easy and fun to read with color coding. Change the font color for each person's remarks as a simple way to identify who is saying what! —*Leah LaMontagne*

Form

SAMPLE LETTER FOR REQUESTING HELP

Sample Letter

[Your Name and Address]

[Date]

[Contact Name and Address]

Dear [Your Relative's Name],

I'm gathering information about our family history, and I recently discovered we are related <explain the relationship further or omit this part if you know the relative>. I am currently working on the <surname> branch of the family and wonder if you could help me. In particular, I am looking for <short list of information that you need, such as names or birth dates of specific people>.

I appreciate you taking the time to pass along any information you may have. I would also love to see copies of any photographs you may have of this branch of the family. If you would like, I would be happy to send you the information I have collected thus far about our family.

Best regards,

<Your Name>

Take good notes.

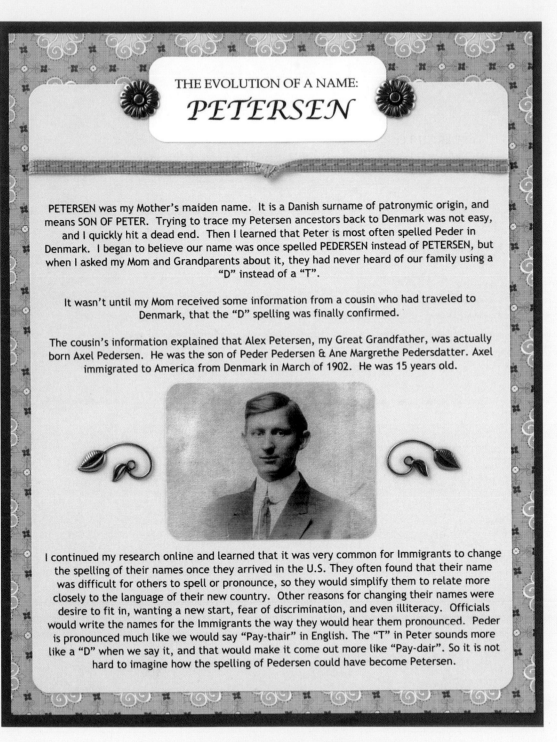

THE EVOLUTION OF A NAME:
PETERSEN

PETERSEN was my Mother's maiden name. It is a Danish surname of patronymic origin, and means SON OF PETER. Trying to trace my Petersen ancestors back to Denmark was not easy, and I quickly hit a dead end. Then I learned that Peter is most often spelled Peder in Denmark. I began to believe our name was once spelled PEDERSEN instead of PETERSEN, but when I asked my Mom and Grandparents about it, they had never heard of our family using a "D" instead of a "T".

It wasn't until my Mom received some information from a cousin who had traveled to Denmark, that the "D" spelling was finally confirmed.

The cousin's information explained that Alex Petersen, my Great Grandfather, was actually born Axel Pedersen. He was the son of Peder Pedersen & Ane Margrethe Pedersdatter. Axel immigrated to America from Denmark in March of 1902. He was 15 years old.

I continued my research online and learned that it was very common for Immigrants to change the spelling of their names once they arrived in the U.S. They often found that their name was difficult for others to spell or pronounce, so they would simplify them to relate more closely to the language of their new country. Other reasons for changing their names were desire to fit in, wanting a new start, fear of discrimination, and even illiteracy. Officials would write the names for the Immigrants the way they would hear them pronounced. Peder is pronounced much like we would say "Pay-thair" in English. The "T" in Peter sounds more like a "D" when we say it, and that would make it come out more like "Pay-dair". So it is not hard to imagine how the spelling of Pedersen could have become Petersen.

The Evolution of a Name: Petersen BY LEAH LaMONTAGNE

Tip: Journal about the process of research and discovery in family history scrapbooking. Include details about how you ran into dead ends, who and where you went to for help, and how you finally found your information. —*Leah LaMontagne*

Form

RESEARCH LOG

RESEARCH LOG

ANCESTOR'S NAME _____ ☐ Male ☐ Female
First   Middle   Last (Maiden/Surname)

Born _____ Married _____ Died _____

SEARCH DATE	SEARCH QUESTION	SOURCE OF INFORMATION	NOTES

Download the full-size version of this form at: *www.creatingkeepsakes.com/familyhistoryworkbook* or *www.leisurearts.com/familyhistory*

Page Planner 1

Use the page planner on the opposite page as a starting point for creating your own scrapbook pages. Here's how Carey used the page planner to tell a favorite family story.

It is obvious that my dad's lifelong love of reading and learning started early. While growing up, I remember many nights when he read to me in bed...the beauty of modeling positive behavior seems to have at least some affect on each generation. This photo belongs in my classroom as a reminder to my high school students and future parents, just how important it is to read to children. My dad turned out pretty darn good, and this quiet moment caught on film in 1948 is just one of the many important reasons why.

Read BY CAREY JOHNSON

Tip: Scan and enlarge a favorite photo to include on a scrapbook page. —*Carey Johnson*

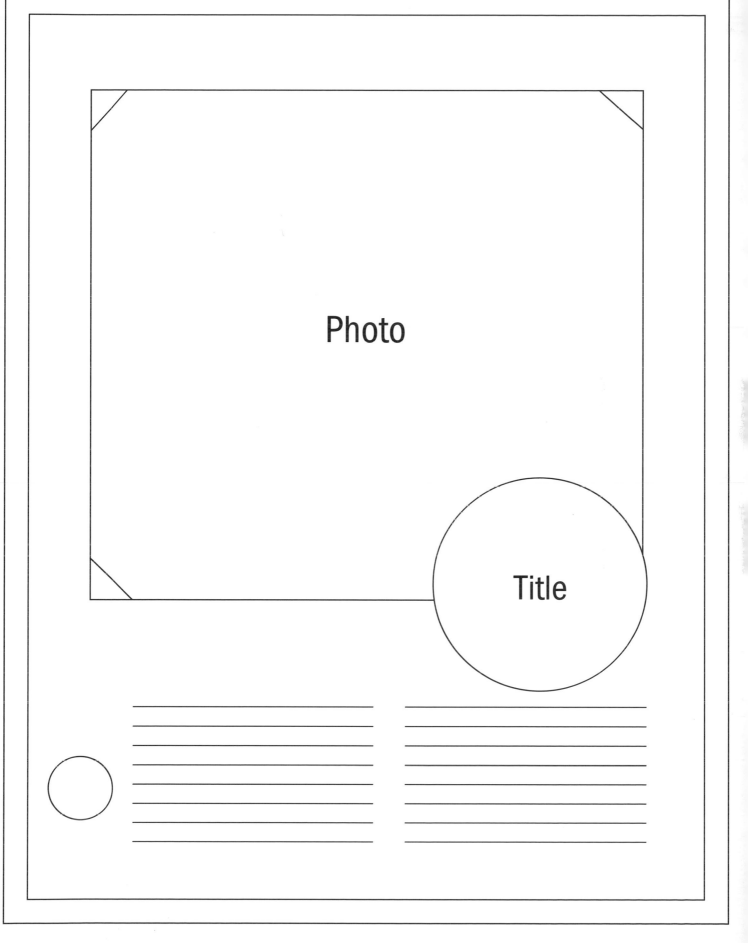

Photo

Title

Use the page planner on the opposite page as a starting point for creating your own scrapbook pages. Here's how Carey used the page planner to tell a favorite family story.

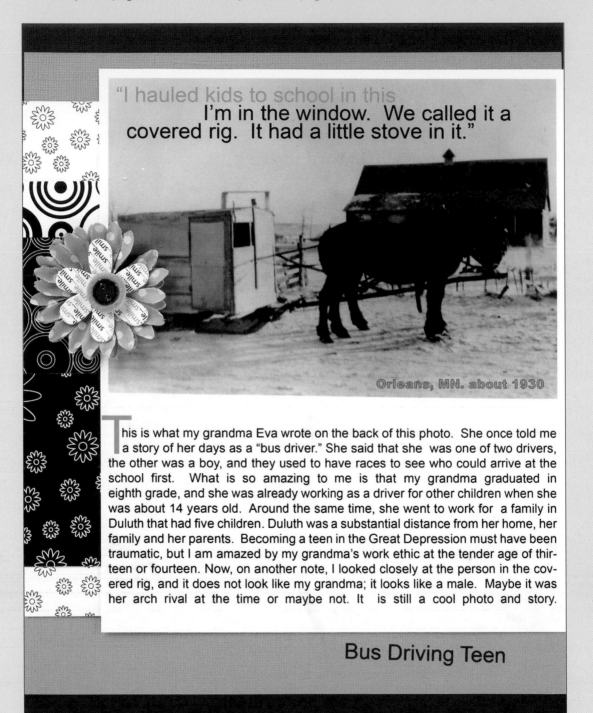

"I hauled kids to school in this I'm in the window. We called it a covered rig. It had a little stove in it."

Orleans, MN. about 1930

This is what my grandma Eva wrote on the back of this photo. She once told me a story of her days as a "bus driver." She said that she was one of two drivers, the other was a boy, and they used to have races to see who could arrive at the school first.   What is so amazing to me is that my grandma graduated in eighth grade, and she was already working as a driver for other children when she was about 14 years old. Around the same time, she went to work for a family in Duluth that had five children. Duluth was a substantial distance from her home, her family and her parents. Becoming a teen in the Great Depression must have been traumatic, but I am amazed by my grandma's work ethic at the tender age of thirteen or fourteen. Now, on another note, I looked closely at the person in the covered rig, and it does not look like my grandma; it looks like a male. Maybe it was her arch rival at the time or maybe not. It   is still a cool photo and story.

Bus Driving Teen

Bus-Driving Teen BY CAREY JOHNSON

Tip: This is a story I always wanted to tell about my grandma. I wish I would have asked her to tell me all of these stories and tape-recorded them so they would be preserved. Now I just have to rely on memory.
—*Carey Johnson*

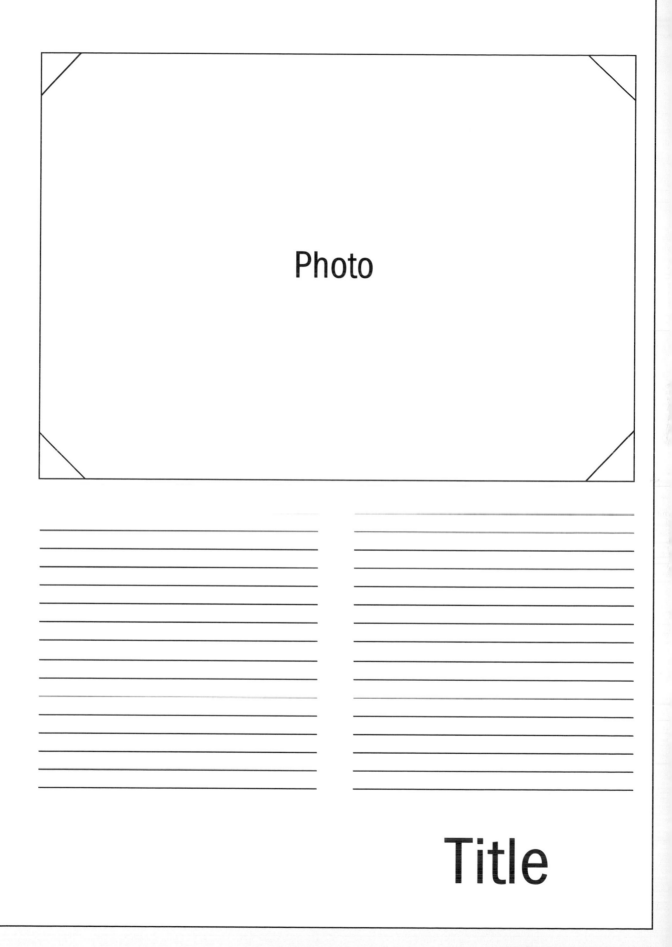

Photo

Title

Family Album
Q&A with Amanda Probst

When We Were Your Age . . . BY AMANDA PROBST

Why did you decide to create this album?

My boys often complain that certain things aren't "fair," so I decided they should know just how leisurely their lives are in comparison to their ancestors' lives. This way, when they start complaining about not wanting to do their chores, I can whip this album out and show them what sorts of chores their grandparents and great-grandparents did.

Why is this album important to you?

I love to record my family's stories and feel that childhood is often overlooked in heritage projects, though we focus so much on it in our current albums.

Is this a stand-alone album or part of a series?

I think this album will stand alone, though I'd love to come up with other question topics to address. It seems to be easier to get relatives to help out by asking for small bits of information rather than overwhelming them with asking for "everything" all at once.

When (and where) were you born?
January 8, 1950; St. Elizabeth Hospital, Yakima, WA

Do you know any stories about your birth and infancy?
Richard and I were healthy babies; neither twin was fragile. I was a good baby, the more outgoing of the twins – the bravest per Grams. Both of us were active but we didn't fight with each other. When I was 3 yrs. old, I was run over by a car. According to Grams, a slew of kids were playing around the produce stand near our home on Lateral A. It was a very busy evening (September, Labor Day weekend) with cars going in and out. Grams was worried that someone was going to get hurt so she started chasing all the kids away from the stand - with a box slat in hand – and into the house. A customer started talking to her about tomatoes and she stopped chasing us and the next thing she heard was a bump. Then she saw Aunt Nemie DeFiesta (who lived in another house on the property) run and pick me up and bring me to her. She thinks I'd sat down on the ground in front of the car (middle part) to put on my sandal/shoe. The man didn't see me and ran over me but due to the fact that I had possibly rolled under the car from the wheels, he drove over the fleshy part of my calf. The front bumper had hit my forehead so I had a bruise/bump. They took me to the doctor in Yakima and had a pelvic x-ray to make sure that I didn't have any internal injuries (no head x-ray done). Grams stayed overnight in the hospital with me. The next day she carried me around all day; said she didn't put me down at all and that her arms were very tired and sore. The man that ran over me felt very bad and paid the doctor and hospital bill. Of course, since I wasn't a fragile child (like your father, Robert) I recuperated quickly. Dad was upset and blamed mom for not keeping a closer eye on us.

How did your parents choose your name?
My first name is from mom's mother; middle name is after the nun that helped deliver me.

How many brothers and sisters did you have? (and where did you fall in the line up?)
My twin brother, Richard, and I were the youngest (though I was the older twin). We had one older sister and one older brother.

What games did you like to play as a kid?
Hide and Seek, Mother May I, London Bridge, Ring Around the Rosie, jump rope, Old Maid, checkers, puzzles, tag, rope pulls, tree climbing, yo-yos, ride bikes, rotten tomato fights, football, jacks, hopscotch, dodgeball, baseball. To make things more fun and the time go by faster, Richard and I usually made a game out of whatever farm work we had to do. Dad wasn't big on buying toys or board games. I had dolls, but the first doll that was bought only for me was when I got out of the hospital after my tonsillitis surgery. Believe I was 9 and Aunt Helen Baldoz bought it for me.

What did you learn?
I went to Parker Elementary from 1st to 6th grade. There was one room for each grade; it was part of the Wapato School District. Besides the 3 R's we also had lessons in history, social studies, art, music, geography, nutrition, and science. Absolutely enjoyed school – always interesting and fun (plus while at school, I didn't have to work on the farm). I especially loved my 5th and 6th grade teachers, Mrs. Storvic (her great aunt was Harriet Beecher Stowe) and Mr. Olson, respectively. It was rare to have a man teacher then, but Mr. Olson was great; he taught me discipline and how to become a better person; he always seemed to believe in me and challenged me. Another teacher I liked was our music/art teacher, Mrs. Dunn. She was nice to me and encouraged me to sing. I remember one Christmas Program that we had at school. Our class sang The 12 days of Christmas and I got to do the 5 Golden Rings part – I thought I was pretty hot stuff. I was really bummed when in the 7th grade (Wapato Jr. High) my brother got her for his homeroom teacher and I got Mrs. Garrett (hated her with a passion). I tried to ask dad to transfer me to Mrs. Dunn, but since Richard was in there, they said siblings couldn't be together. Honestly, I would have taken any other homeroom teacher versus Mrs. Garrett – that was one strange lady! However, that's a whole different story.

What did you want to be when you grew up?
Opera Singer

What sorts of things did you do around the house (chores)?
Ironed, dusted, helped with cooking, set the table, washed dishes, swept/mopped, yard work, and worked in the fields from March to November.

How did you get to school?
Rode the bus. We were one of first families on. I liked riding except for one time when Richard and I had been playing on our swing and I fell off and hit my head on the ground. I felt dizzy throughout the whole ride; when I finally got off the bus at school, I threw up. We lived about a mile and a half from school, could have caught the bus at the end of its run, but dad didn't want us walking the ¼ mile to the pick up point. However, on the last of school (I think when we were 6th graders), we did get to walk all the way to school – thought that was pretty cool.

Did you like school?
Loved Parker Elementary. Disliked most of the 7th grade year (Mrs. Garrett's class only), 8th & 9th were fun. High school was high school . . .

Did you have a chance to play with cousins very often?
When our first cousins (Uncle Primo's kids) lived on a farm a few miles away from us, we saw them often. When they moved to town and became city folk, we didn't see them as much ...usually only at the hall. Most of the time we saw our first, second and third cousins during the holidays or at the hall. We mostly played with the kids that lived in the houses next to us and a family that lived down the road.

What do you remember most about your grandparents?
I didn't know my grandparents on either side. Dad's parents were in the Philippines; mom's father was deceased. Mom's mother lived in Yakima, but I was too young to remember (I was 3 when she died).

mary

Oct 1958: Remy, Mary & Delores-Seattle, WA

c. 1960s: Mary, Delores & Richard-Parker, WA

How long did your project take?

The pages themselves didn't take very long at all to create—maybe 30–60 minutes (depending on the amount of journaling) for each person featured. I kept the design simple to focus on the story.

What's your best advice on family history scrapbooking?

Start small. It's easy to get overwhelmed with family history projects. Pick a single topic (like childhood) and come up with just a handful of questions. It's amazing how much more cooperation you'll get when the task seems smaller.

chapter 2

Family

"In every conceivable manner, the family is link to our past,
bridge to our future." — *Alex Haley*

This is a photo of one of the family trees I drew & gave as Christmas gifts in 2000. I made them while waiting for Noah's birth.

{ **family tree** }

Family Tree BY AMANDA PROBST

Tip: Family trees are tricky creatures—either they're too huge to fit on a page or too full of holes to merit one. As a solution, I drew my own family tree and included it on my page. —*Amanda Probst*

Form

PHOTO FAMILY TREE

FIVE-GENERATION PICTURE PEDIGREE CHART

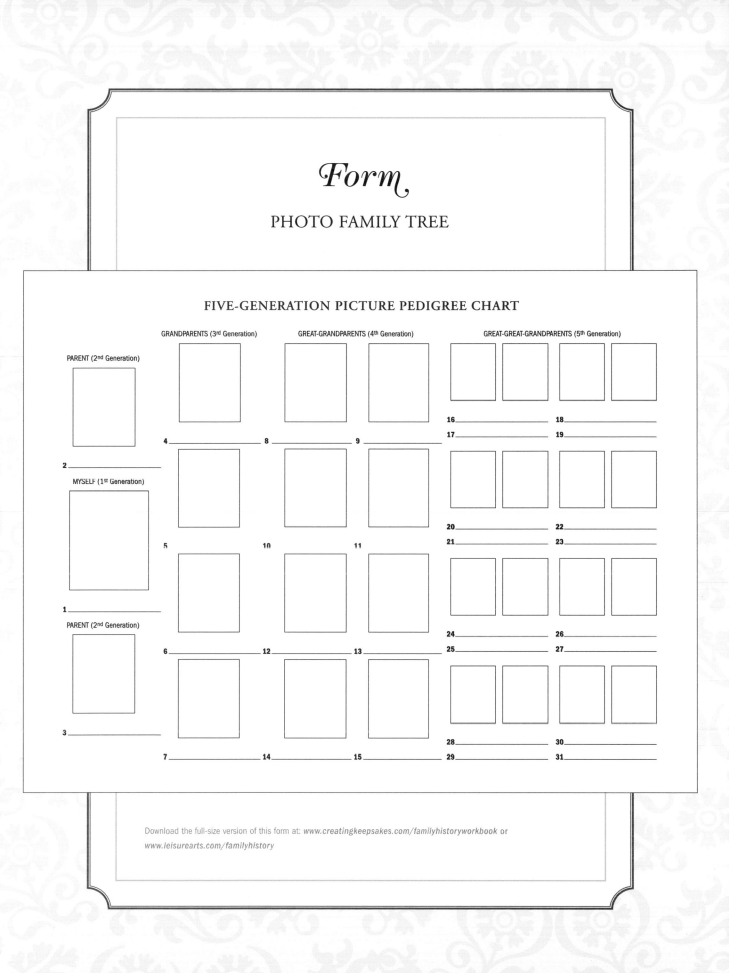

PARENT (2nd Generation)

GRANDPARENTS (3rd Generation)

GREAT-GRANDPARENTS (4th Generation)

GREAT-GREAT-GRANDPARENTS (5th Generation)

16 _____ 18 _____
17 _____ 19 _____

2 _____

MYSELF (1st Generation)

4 _____ 8 _____ 9 _____

20 _____ 22 _____
21 _____ 23 _____

5 _____ 10 _____ 11 _____

1 _____

PARENT (2nd Generation)

24 _____ 26 _____
25 _____ 27 _____

6 _____ 12 _____ 13 _____

3 _____

28 _____ 30 _____
29 _____ 31 _____

7 _____ 14 _____ 15 _____

Scrapbook a pedigree chart.

Stephen Michael 12-25-1909 6-3-1979 — **Ann Josephine** 3-28-1909 11-11-1955

m. 11-17-1938

| Ann Marie 11-28-1940 | Catherine Patricia 3-17-1942 | Stephen Michael 8-21-1943 | Thomas Joseph 9-18-1945 | Barbara Jean 8-6-1947 | James Paul 11-14-1948 5-12-1993 | Rose Mary 12-2-1949 | Robert Edward 12-2-1949 |

m. Matthew Ferriole 6-25-1966 — m. Thomas Beebe 9-5-1970 — m. Lillian Goode 2-8-1964 — m. Jeanene Jones 8-21-1971 — m. Ronald Tweiten 7-14-1973 — m. Richard Dorsett 12-18-1971 — m. Mary Baldoz 6-17-1972

SMITH COUSINS

Mary Ann 7-24-1967 — Jon Thomas 4-8-1971 — Stephen Michael 1-1-1965 5-25-2006 — Jason Thomas 1-14-1975 — Michael Alan 10-9-1975 — Richard Allen 4-2-1975 — Amanda Ni Eun 6-7-1975

Tina Marie 4-1-1971 — Katherine Marlene 8-15-1968 — April Elizabeth 2-26-1976 — Jeffery Paul 4-30-1977 — Matthew John 6-2-1977 — Zachary Robert 3-16-1979

Jennifer Elizabeth 10-4-1969 — Adam Patrick 9-26-1978 — Jo Ann 8-24-1980 — David Allen 11-30-1978 — Rebekah Marie 4-20-1982

Anthony Joseph 10-27-1970 — Elizabeth Ann 1-23-1982 — Joseph Roy 3-28-1983

Gregory Paul 11-3-1983 — Cassandra Renee 9-11-1984

Michelle Renee 2-14-1989

Anthony James 8-19-1991

partial group photo July 29, 1995... Yakima, WA

Smith Cousins BY AMANDA PROBST

Tip: I wanted to do a slightly different take on the family tree to include cousins rather than just ancestors. This grid paper worked perfectly, allowing me to cut small blocks of cardstock, label them and place them as shown. —*Amanda Probst*

Form

PEDIGREE CHART

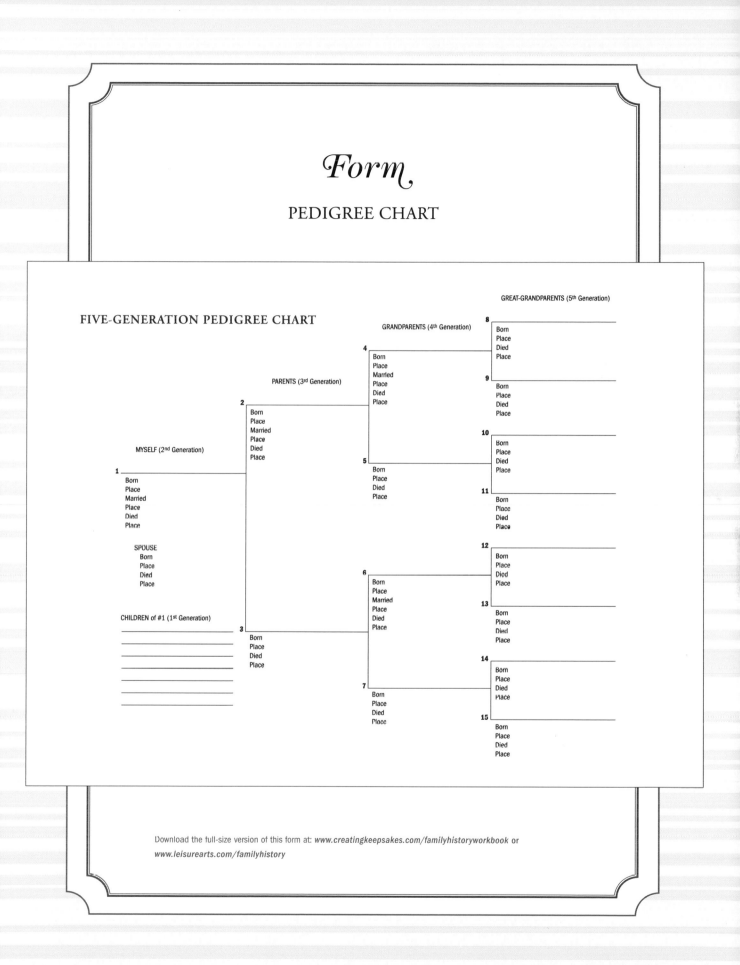

FIVE-GENERATION PEDIGREE CHART

GREAT-GRANDPARENTS (5th Generation)

GRANDPARENTS (4th Generation)

PARENTS (3rd Generation)

MYSELF (2nd Generation)

1
Born
Place
Married
Place
Died
Place

SPOUSE
Born
Place
Died
Place

CHILDREN of #1 (1st Generation)

2
Born
Place
Married
Place
Died
Place

3
Born
Place
Died
Place

4
Born
Place
Married
Place
Died
Place

5
Born
Place
Died
Place

6
Born
Place
Married
Place
Died
Place

7
Born
Place
Died
Place

8
Born
Place
Died
Place

9
Born
Place
Died
Place

10
Born
Place
Died
Place

11
Born
Place
Died
Place

12
Born
Place
Died
Place

13
Born
Place
Died
Place

14
Born
Place
Died
Place

15
Born
Place
Died
Place

Download the full-size version of this form at: *www.creatingkeepsakes.com/familyhistoryworkbook* or *www.leisurearts.com/familyhistory*

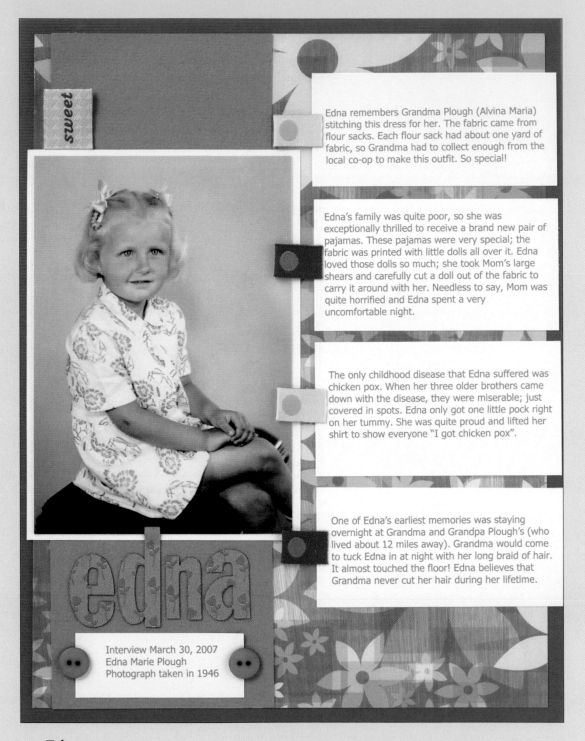

sweet

Edna remembers Grandma Plough (Alvina Maria) stitching this dress for her. The fabric came from flour sacks. Each flour sack had about one yard of fabric, so Grandma had to collect enough from the local co-op to make this outfit. So special!

Edna's family was quite poor, so she was exceptionally thrilled to receive a brand new pair of pajamas. These pajamas were very special; the fabric was printed with little dolls all over it. Edna loved those dolls so much; she took Mom's large shears and carefully cut a doll out of the fabric to carry it around with her. Needless to say, Mom was quite horrified and Edna spent a very uncomfortable night.

The only childhood disease that Edna suffered was chicken pox. When her three older brothers came down with the disease, they were miserable; just covered in spots. Edna only got one little pock right on her tummy. She was quite proud and lifted her shirt to show everyone "I got chicken pox".

One of Edna's earliest memories was staying overnight at Grandma and Grandpa Plough's (who lived about 12 miles away). Grandma would come to tuck Edna in at night with her long braid of hair. It almost touched the floor! Edna believes that Grandma never cut her hair during her lifetime.

edna

Interview March 30, 2007
Edna Marie Plough
Photograph taken in 1946

Edna BY KIM KESTI

Tip: Since I wanted to include a variety of memories on one layout, I separated each story onto its own journaling tag for clarity. —*Kim Kesti*

Worksheet

INDIVIDUAL INTERVIEW FORM

1. What is your full name, including your maiden name? Do you have any nicknames?

   ....
   ....
   ....

2. When and where were you born? How did your family come to live there?

   ....
   ....
   ....

3. When and where were you married? What is the most memorable moment from your wedding day?

   ....
   ....
   ....

4. How many children do you have? What was being a new parent like for you?

   ....
   ....
   ....

5. Write about your childhood. What is one of your favorite childhood memories?

   ....
   ....
   ....

Journal about a family member.

A measure of love…

I was thrilled when Great Aunt Martha gave me a copy of this photo. I had never seen it before and it brought back such good memories of Great Grandma. I asked my Mom and Grandma to journal about Fannie, too. It's sweet to have three generations of memories documented here. (Journaling done on March 28, 2007, Photo of Fannie Ottila Koivisto taken in 1968)

While growing up in Minnesota my grandmother lived 2 houses away. She didn't speak English and I would do small errands for her. Every Saturday she would give me a "Saturday Nickel" — your granddaughter

WHAT LIFE WAS LIKE

BEFORE MOTHERHOOD.

DESCRIPTION

I remember my mother washing clothes in the house and she had lots of clothes for she had 10 children. During the depression my mother made meat balls on Sunday for a special treat

DATE: Your daughter No. 345

favorite.

DESCRIPTION

I remember Great Grandma's beautiful braids — I never saw her without them. I used to sit with her in church and happily dig in her big black purse. She always had pink peppermints and a real linen hanky. I wish I remember more about her.

DATE: Memories of the 100%— great granddaughter

A Measure of Love BY KIM KESTI

Tip: I wanted this layout to have a very personal feel, so I had each family member journal in his or her own handwriting. —*Kim Kesti*

Checklist

STORY STARTERS

Wondering what stories to share? Look at the pages in this workbook for ideas, or journal about one of these topics:

- **Adventures.** Did your family member have an adventurous spirit? What sort of risks did he take? Did he travel to any exotic locations?

- **Belongings.** What belongings do you always associate with a certain family member? Did a female family member always carry a certain type of gum or mints in her purse?

- **Books.** Did a family member love to read? Did he have a preferred genre, like westerns or mysteries? Did he read the newspaper every morning?

- **Games.** Does your family have a history of enjoying a certain type of game, like board games, card games or word games?

- **Handwriting.** Was a family member known for his handwriting? Was it distinctive, neat or messy?

- **Routines.** Did your family member have a certain beauty routine, like brushing her hair a hundred times a night or always wearing her hair in braids?

Interview a group of family members.

Boy Meets Girl BY SHELLEY LAMING

Tip: This is a layout about two young people falling in love, so I wanted to use products that had an element of fun. Just because you're scrapping heritage photos doesn't mean you can't use contemporary products. —*Shelley Laming*

Worksheet

FAMILY INTERVIEW FORM

1. What do you know about your family surname, including its origin and meaning?

   ....

   ....

   ....

2. What stories do you know about your parents? Grandparents? Other distant relatives?

   ....

   ....

   ....

3. What historical events have impacted your family? For instance, how did your family survive the Depression? What national conflicts, such as the Civil War or other more recent events, have affected your family? How?

   ....

   ....

   ....

4. What holidays are most important in your family, and how do you celebrate them?

   ....

   ....

   ....

5. Where does your family keep photo albums, scrapbooks, slides or home movies?

   ....

   ....

   ....

tall oaks from little acorns grow.

"ned"

Ned was born Thomas Edwin Laming but has always gone by his nickname. He was named after Paps' uncle, who also used "Ned" as a nickname. Ned is proud to carry on the name of his great uncle.

Ned BY SHELLEY LAMING

Tip: Don't be afraid to mix two totally different types of photos on one layout. Here, one photo is color and the other is black and white, but also, one is a snapshot and the other is a school portrait. —*Shelley Laming*

Form

FAMILY NAMES

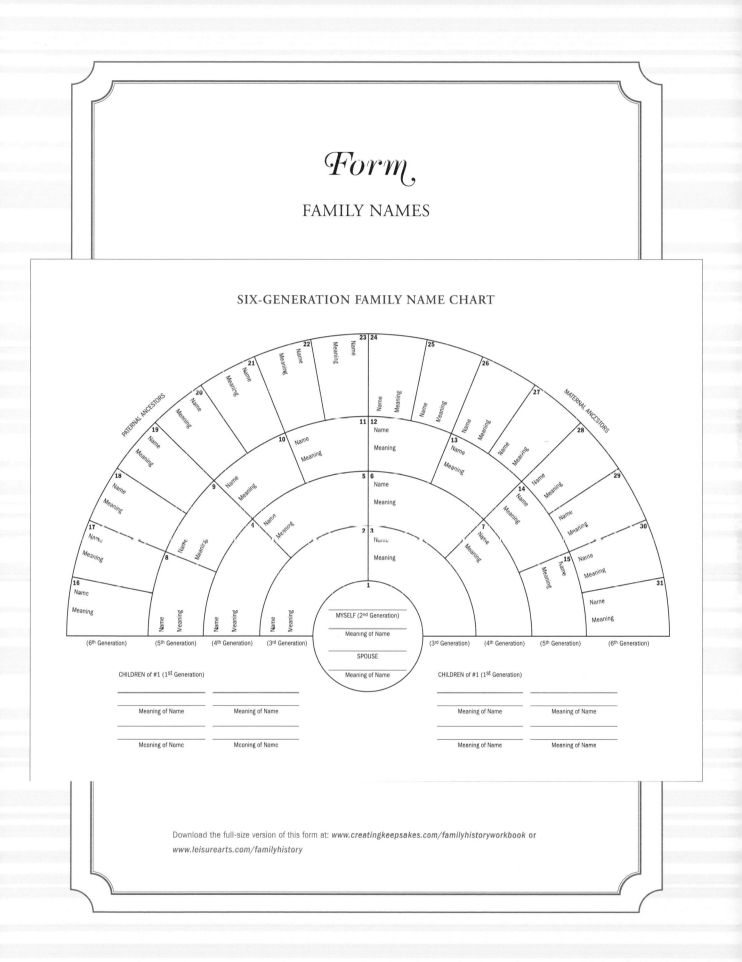

SIX-GENERATION FAMILY NAME CHART

PATERNAL ANCESTORS

MATERNAL ANCESTORS

23	24	25
22 Name / Meaning		26
21 Name / Meaning		27
20 Name / Meaning	11 / 12 Name / Meaning	28
19 Name / Meaning	10 Name / Meaning	13 Name / Meaning
18 Name / Meaning	9 Name / Meaning	5 / 6 Name / Meaning	14 Name / Meaning	29
17 Name / Meaning	4 Name / Meaning	2 / 3 Name / Meaning	7 Name / Meaning	30
8 Name / Meaning		15 Name / Meaning	31
16 Name / Meaning		Name / Meaning

1

MYSELF (2nd Generation)

Meaning of Name

SPOUSE

Meaning of Name

(6th Generation) (5th Generation) (4th Generation) (3rd Generation)   (3rd Generation) (4th Generation) (5th Generation) (6th Generation)

CHILDREN of #1 (1st Generation)

_____   _____
Meaning of Name   Meaning of Name
_____   _____
Meaning of Name   Meaning of Name

CHILDREN of #1 (1st Generation)

_____   _____
Meaning of Name   Meaning of Name
_____   _____
Meaning of Name   Meaning of Name

Download the full-size version of this form at: *www.creatingkeepsakes.com/familyhistoryworkbook* or
www.leisurearts.com/familyhistory

Family
TRADITIONS

When my grandmother was growing up there were not many career options for women. If they worked at all, it was either as a teacher or a nurse. My grandmother did both. She went to school first to become a teacher. Then, for reasons unknown to me, she went back to school after teaching third grade for a couple of years to become a nurse.

She worked as a nurse until she married and had children. When I was in college I was bound and determined to break out of the "women only" tradition. But low and behold, my major in college was nursing. I've been working as a labor and delivery nurse for the past 17 years. When I chose my major I decided that nursing would be a great career to have and still be able to raise a family. I believe those family values came in large part from my grandmother. My sister followed in this family tradition as well. She became an operating room nurse. I love seeing the influence of my grandmother passed down through the generations.

Lucile
Trumbull
circa 1930

Family Traditions BY VICKI HARVEY

Worksheet

FAMILY TRAITS

1. What is a classic family trait? How has that trait been manifested as the family has grown?

   ....

   ....

   ....

2. What are a few common physical family attributes? Are they liked or disliked? What jokes surround certain characteristics?

   ....

   ....

   ....

3. What talents, skills or hobbies are shared within the family?

   ....

   ....

   ....

4. What distinctive personality characteristics are unique to the family? Who exhibits the behavior most, and who is the most lacking in the behavior?

   ....

   ....

   ....

5. What funny family stories surround common family traits?

   ....

   ....

   ....

Lucile - early 1930's

There are some stories in my family's history that are not documented. I've learned about them by talking to my Great Uncle Lelynn. Apparently my grandmother was engaged to a man named Harold before she met my grandfather. She was going to nursing school when she met Harold. They became engaged and she moved home to plan the wedding. The big day arrived and Harold never showed up. She never heard from him again. It is so puzzling to me why this man would abandon my grandmother like that. She was such an amazing woman. She was educated, a seamstress, a great cook and very handy. It's hard to believe that anyone could be so cruel. But, had this twist of fate never happened, I wouldn't be here. So, in a strange way, I have to be grateful to Harold.

Why?

Why? BY VICKI HARVEY

Tip: Talk to family members about their memories. You may discover things you would have never known otherwise. —*Vicki Harvey*

Worksheet

FAMILY STORIES—TRUTH OR FICTION?

1. What is a favorite family story that seems to have many different versions, depending on who tells the story? Which version seems to be the most common?

   ....

   ....

   ....

2. Can you locate journals or a family Bible that may offer more accurate information about the story?

   ....

   ....

   ....

3. Are there living relatives who were present at the time the events in the story took place? If so, contact each individual and conduct a short interview to get more concrete details.

   ....

   ....

   ....

4. Record several versions of the story along a simple timeline. Look for discrepancies. Is there a way to resolve the mystery details by eliminating the facts you know are false?

   ....

   ....

   ....

5. If the story surrounds a national event, look for additional information sources that could support or deny the validity of the story, such as newspaper accounts or historical records.

   ....

   ....

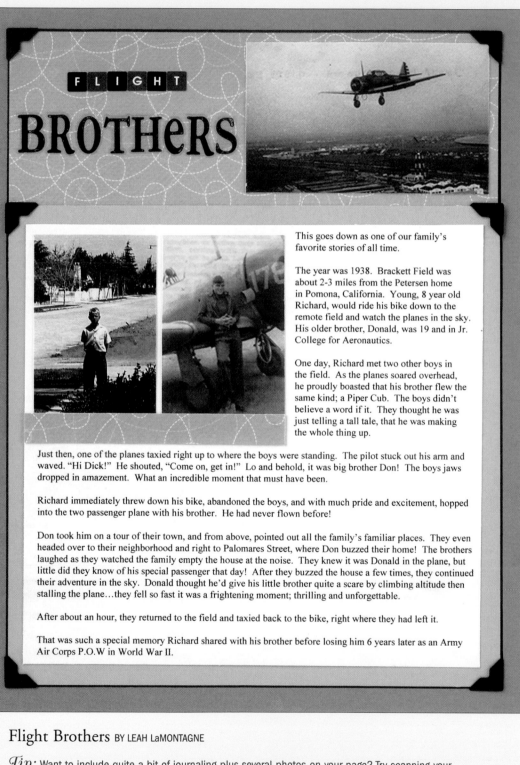

FLIGHT

BROTHERS

This goes down as one of our family's favorite stories of all time.

The year was 1938. Brackett Field was about 2-3 miles from the Petersen home in Pomona, California. Young, 8 year old Richard, would ride his bike down to the remote field and watch the planes in the sky. His older brother, Donald, was 19 and in Jr. College for Aeronautics.

One day, Richard met two other boys in the field. As the planes soared overhead, he proudly boasted that his brother flew the same kind; a Piper Cub. The boys didn't believe a word if it. They thought he was just telling a tall tale, that he was making the whole thing up.

Just then, one of the planes taxied right up to where the boys were standing. The pilot stuck out his arm and waved. "Hi Dick!" He shouted, "Come on, get in!" Lo and behold, it was big brother Don! The boys jaws dropped in amazement. What an incredible moment that must have been.

Richard immediately threw down his bike, abandoned the boys, and with much pride and excitement, hopped into the two passenger plane with his brother. He had never flown before!

Don took him on a tour of their town, and from above, pointed out all the family's familiar places. They even headed over to their neighborhood and right to Palomares Street, where Don buzzed their home! The brothers laughed as they watched the family empty the house at the noise. They knew it was Donald in the plane, but little did they know of his special passenger that day! After they buzzed the house a few times, they continued their adventure in the sky. Donald thought he'd give his little brother quite a scare by climbing altitude then stalling the plane…they fell so fast it was a frightening moment; thrilling and unforgettable.

After about an hour, they returned to the field and taxied back to the bike, right where they had left it.

That was such a special memory Richard shared with his brother before losing him 6 years later as an Army Air Corps P.O.W in World War II.

Flight Brothers BY LEAH LaMONTAGNE

Tip: Want to include quite a bit of journaling plus several photos on your page? Try scanning your photographs and printing them in a smaller size. —*Leah LaMontagne*

Worksheet

FAVORITE FAMILY STORIES

1. Who first told you this story, and what version were you told?

   _____

   _____

   _____

   _____

2. What unanswered questions do you have about the story?

   _____

   _____

   _____

   _____

3. What individuals could you talk with to get more information about the story?

   _____

   _____

   _____

   _____

4. What is your favorite part of the story? Why is it your favorite?

   _____

   _____

   _____

   _____

5. When you retell the story, what version will you tell?

   _____

   _____

   _____

   _____

Solve a photo mystery.

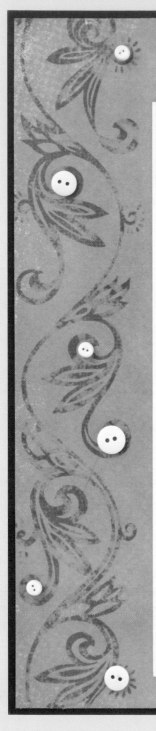

DONALD MALONE

The little information I can document on the life of Donald Malone has come from Jerry's Grandfather, Gene Goosman, who was a cousin to Donald.

Donald was the son of Pearl (Ola's oldest sister) & Herman Malone. He had one brother named Russell. Donald was born around 1922 in Nevada, Iowa. He probably had a childhood much like Gene did as a boy, since they were close in age and both grew up in the same town.

The U.S. entered World War II in 1941, and sometime after that Donald joined the Navy. He would have been around 18 years old. A few years later the war was over and he had not yet been discharged. His ship stopped in San Francisco and the Sailors were out on shore leave when tragedy took place. Donald's young life came to an end when he was hit by a street car. Gene thinks he was about 22 or 23 years old when he died.

I found this picture in a box of photos from Jerry's Grandma Kay. Donald is on the right. I'm sure it was taken during his travels with the Navy, and the man with him was probably a friend he served with. Other than that, nobody can tell exactly where or when the picture was taken. The building behind them is beautiful, but I suppose its identity will remain a mystery.

Donald Malone BY LEAH LaMONTAGNE

Tip: Don't worry when you come across a photograph you can't identify. Use what details you have and add common knowledge and information from other resources, like the Internet and books. It's also okay to say, "This photo is a bit of a mystery" on your scrapbook page. —*Leah LaMontagne*

Checklist

IDENTIFY MYSTERY PHOTOGRAPHS

☐ Look for the date.
It's common to find a date printed in the margin on the back of a photograph. You may need to hold it up to the light, use a magnifying glass or scan the back of the photo and enhance the image to see the date.

☐ Study the clothing and setting in the photograph. Take note of military uniforms.
Many websites and reference books provide examples of traditional dress and styles for different time periods. Do a web search using key words such as "18th century clothing" and "photodating," or visit your local library for books that date historical costume.

☐ Research the type of photo.
Each photo (daguerreotypes, ambrotypes, carte-de-visites [cdvs] cabinets, tintypes, stereotypes, snapshots, postcards, etc.) were taken in a certain time period in which that photographic method was most likely used. You'll find many books with extensive information on this subject at your local library or historical center.

☐ Take note of automobiles in the photo.
A vehicle's license plate will not only tell you the location, but may also help you trace the owner of the vehicle. (Check with a historical society or library.)

☐ Send a photocopied version of the photograph to or visit people who might know something about the individual(s) in the photograph.
If it's a group photo, ask the individuals to write the names of the people they know on the photocopied version and mail it back to you. Be sure to include a self-addressed, stamped envelope.

Note:
Don't make photocopies of daguerreotypes, tintypes, glass-plate negatives and some older photographs because they are light sensitive and can be damaged. Check with your local library for books about handling older photographs.

Page Planner 3

Use the page planner on the opposite page as a starting point for creating your own scrapbook pages. Here's how Carey used the page planner to tell a favorite family story.

The Studio is not only where my grandparents worked, but it's also where they lived. It is where they raised their children; it is where they played with their grandchildren. It is where they entertained their friends and family; it is where they created. I have many memories of The Studio. I remember the big old ornate chair; I remember the portraits of each of us hanging above the counter that where photographed by my grandpa and then oil painted over by my grandma; I remember the big heavy red curtains that hung in the back that we used to play behind; I remember jumping from the old window in the music room onto the sofa below; I remember the makeup vanity that my grandma would use to touch up clients; I remember the box of toys used for entertaining fickle children. I remember hanging plants, a big old large format camera, scary darkrooms and basements, "look at my nose", wonderful smells from the kitchen, a fireplace that didn't work, floral orange curtains, oil paints, licking my lips for photos, round chairs, beautiful built-ins, dark wood, creepy attics with tons of games, records and toys that belonged to my dad, locks on the cabinets, grandma's pig collection, army men in the neighbor's sandbox, Grandma's sewing machine, German chocolate cake, the old telephone in the nook,...ad infinitum. It is strange, but I still have dreams about the studio. They are often a little melancholy...not scary or really sad, just bittersweet. I dream that my grandparents are still alive; I dream that I am living in the studio/house; I dream that I am confused at being there because I know they are gone, but I am still glad to be there. Those dreams always disturb me a little, but I am glad that I get to revisit a place from my childhood; I get to reconnect to my grandparents in at least some small way & in some small place..

The Studio BY CAREY JOHNSON

Tip: I included unrelated photos that were taken at different times at my grandpa's studio. —*Carey Johnson*

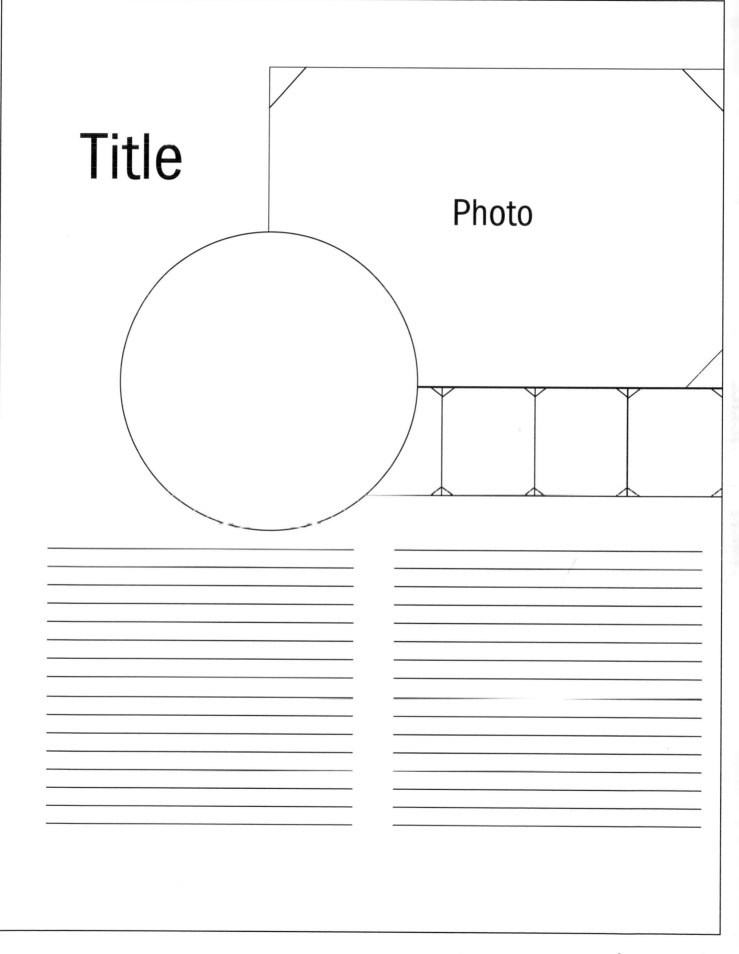

Title

Photo

Page Planner 4

Use the page planner on the opposite page as a starting point for creating your own scrapbook pages. Here's how Carey used the page planner to tell a favorite family story.

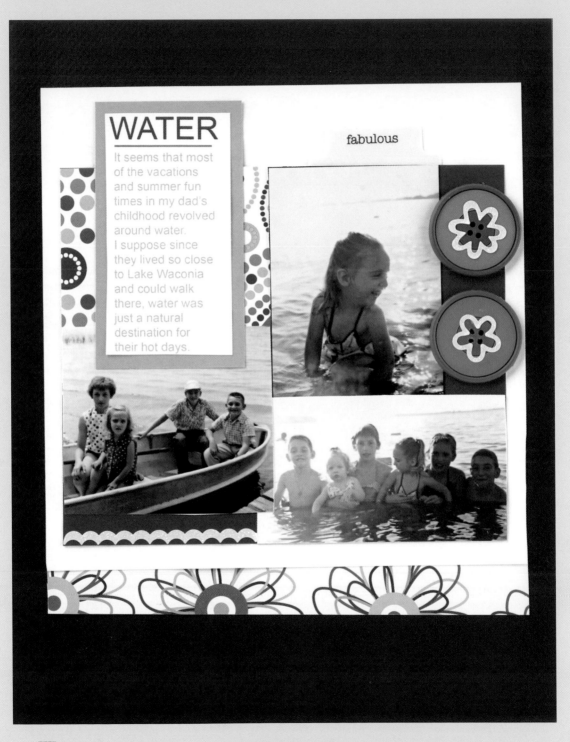

WATER

It seems that most of the vacations and summer fun times in my dad's childhood revolved around water. I suppose since they lived so close to Lake Waconia and could walk there, water was just a natural destination for their hot days.

fabulous

Water BY CAREY JOHNSON

Tip: I thought these photos looked like they could have been taken now instead of 50 years ago, so I gave the layout a fresh and modern look with a lot of white space. I love the bright, fun feel. —*Carey Johnson*

Title

Photo

Photo

Photo

Family Album

Q&A with Kim Kesti

Generations of Love BY KIM KESTI

Why did you decide to create this album?

I've scrapbooked many heritage photos in the past, but I always hesitated to scrapbook wedding photos. They're so special, and I really wanted to display them properly. This album gave me the chance to do that.

Generations of Love

1900's

1940's

1960's

1980's

Why is this album important to you?

I love the broad timeframe of this album—it allows me to share with my children four generations of wedding photos in one compact album. It's also fun to look for similarities in the photos.

Is this a stand-alone album or part of a series?

This is a stand-alone album.

Einar Koivisto and Fannie Ottila Koivisto ⟶ ⟶ United in Matrimony July 25, 1912

How long did your project take?

This album follows a simple template, so it was quite quick to complete. I would estimate that it took three hours to complete the cover, the table of contents and two double-page spreads. I completed each additional page in about 30 minutes.

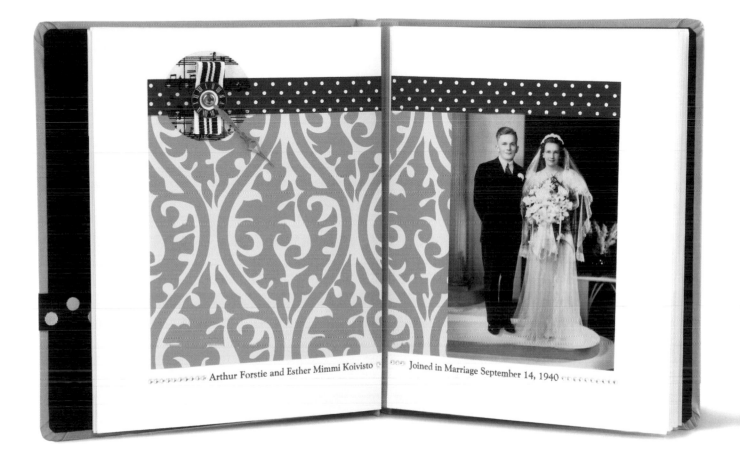

Arthur Forstie and Esther Mimmi Koivisto — Joined in Marriage September 14, 1940

What's your best advice on family history scrapbooking?

Keep your layout template fairly simple. Classic, elegant design will stand the test of time. But classic doesn't have to be boring. I chose patterned papers that are fresh and crisp but have a timeless appeal.

chapter 3

Babies

"A baby is God's opinion that the world should go on."
— *Carl Sandburg*

Record a "we're expecting" story.

twins

Mary & Richard, 8 months old, 1950...Yakima, WA

Twins apparently run in the family. At least they did for my Grandma Robertson (you call her Gramma Robbie). Her youngest children (your Nana Mary and her brother Richard) came about five minutes apart. Grandma claims she wasn't particularly thrilled about the pregnancy until she found out it was twins. This was her fourth pregnancy, and by June she had her suspicions that she was carrying twins (says she could feel two heads) but didn't share that with anyone. In November, the doctor confirmed this. Her due date was January 18, though, which worried her some since her firstborn (Ronald) had died in infancy in January from pneumonia (he was three months old). She, therefore, wasn't in any hurry for the twins to be born, knowing that the longer they made it the better their odds were. She'd had morning sickness during the first trimester and couldn't stand the smell or taste of coffee during any of her pregnancies. (She's a regular coffee drinker.) Grandma says, also, that she had a hard time toward the end with getting around (and up), but she made it to within two weeks of her due date (10 days actually) and managed to deliver naturally. When they were born, she claims there was no celebrating, just back to life as usual. (She laughed when asked.) Apparently, the twins were very good babies.

Twins BY AMANDA PROBST

Tip: The journaling for this layout was difficult because interviewing my grandma wasn't easy. She seemed reluctant to share any details. Fortunately, though, she's still around to share some information.

—Amanda Probst

Worksheet

A PREGNANCY STORY

1. When you first discovered you were (or your wife was) going to have a baby, how did you feel?

   ....

   ....

   ....

2. How did you celebrate and share the news with others?

   ....

   ....

   ....

3. What was your doctor's name, and how did you feel about him or her?

   ....

   ....

   ....

4. Describe any complications or problems along the way. What about cravings, sickness or special moments?

   ....

   ....

   ....

5. If you had more than one child, how has each pregnancy compared with the others? Did it get easier or more difficult?

   ....

   ....

   ....

Tell a story about a new child in the family.

from korea

You were actually supposed to arrive in early April of 1976 but you came down with the chicken pox and were detained for over a month. (I cried all the way home the next day. Some friends from work came over for my baby shower and there was no baby. I'll tell you about that another time.) I believe it was May 26th that you floated in to Seattle and we nervously drove from Prosser. I remember calling Holt right before we left Prosser to make sure that you were arriving this time and once again gave them the Ferriole's phone number in case there was another problem.

It was a beautiful day in the Emerald City . . . Aunt Ann and Uncle Matt came with us to the airport (pretty sure they came in there own car). Your flight was scheduled to arrive in the early afternoon; I only remember this because we drove home that same day. Needless to say, we were very nervous and anxious to see our baby girl. We arrived fairly early at the airport and milled around in the shops. I don't remember buying anything, but thought about getting another stuffed animal for you. I had brought a stuffed something with us along with a bus load of all the necessary baby items Holt had instructed us to bring. It seemed like on your flight (have that info some place) there were quite a number of babies, with each one having there own chaperone. Maybe that's why I don't remember talking too much to your chaperone because couples were all around. Either that or I just tuned everybody out because our little girl that we had been waiting for the past two years for was actually here. I vaguely remember our names were on a card that was pinned to your little white outfit. I recognized you before the chaperone even said our names and made a bee line to you. The chaperone no doubt introduced herself, but I just reached out and took you in my arms. (Okay, here come the tears). You let out a bit of a cry, but I just hugged you tighter, said I love you and kissed your cheek and you stopped. If anybody had tried to take you from me, I would have beat them to a pulp. Anyway, dad and I were grinning ear to ear and it seemed like things were going in slow motion. I finally gave you to your dad who was only allowed to hold you ever so briefly cause he looked so nervous I thought he was going to drop you. While dad was holding you, I checked you out a bit . . . big head, funky hair that stood straight up (glad I had that hat), and the most beautiful smile which you gave me as you came back into my arms. Oddly enough I don't remember anyone asking for ID; they just gave you to us and said congratulations. I'm sure we had to go through some screening process since all the new parents were going out in the same direction. I do remember the chaperone saying that all the children on the flight did well and that you didn't cry much. Aunt Ann and Uncle Matt were very supportive and, of course, were in awe of the whole thing and you. I believe dad and I decided on the way home to ask Uncle Matt to be your godfather.

The drive home was uneventful . . . you slept most of the way home in a baby bed that Aunt Delores had given us. It fit perfectly in the backseat and you slept in it even when we got home. We had been informed by Holt to use powdered milk until you could handle whole, so near Ellensburg, you woke up and began crying. As I began fixing your bottle, it slipped and spilled all over me; I quickly made another bottle which you hungrily took.

I don't remember being all that tired when we arrived back in Prosser; I pretty much hovered over you all night or rock-a-byed you in our cane back rocker. Dad, of course, went to bed. I think he went to the farm the next day, but you'll have to ask him.

LOVE you lots, MOM

From Korea BY AMANDA PROBST

Tip: Sometimes journaling about family history is best done in someone else's voice. For this layout, I used my mom's answer to my question, "Tell me about the day you picked me up at the airport" for the journaling. —*Amanda Probst*

Worksheet

OUR CHILD

1. What type of adjustments did you experience when the new child joined your family?

   ....

   ....

   ....

   ....

2. What adjustments did the new family member experience?

   ....

   ....

   ....

   ....

3. What special things did you do together in the early stages of getting to know each other?

   ....

   ....

   ....

   ....

4. What things did it take a while to understand about each other?

   ....

   ....

   ....

   ....

5. What did you learn about each other during this adjustment period?

   ....

   ....

   ....

   ....

Journal about a baby's name.

I was born on October 6, 1942 at St. Joseph Medical Center in Hancock, Michigan. After three boys, my parents, Harry and Edna Plough, were elated with the arrival of a baby girl. After nine days in the hospital, my Mom and I were finally released and sent home to begin life on the farm. First on the agenda was a name for me. Neither parent could think beyond their own names. My Dad made his bid for a namesake: Harriet. My Mom, still in shock over giving birth to a girl said, "She will be Edna Marie". Thus, I was dubbed "Little Edna". That is, until my three older brothers found a nickname horrible enough to satisfy them.
(Journaling by Edna Plough Kesti on March 23, 2007)

Hey, Baby! BY KIM KESTI

Tip: I took the easy way out on this layout—I asked my mother-in-law to write about how she got her name. It's such a fun story, and hearing it in her own words was just the touch I needed for this page. —*Kim Kesti*

Worksheet

A BABY'S NAME

1. What name did you select for your new baby? Why?

   ....

   ....

   ....

   ....

2. What special meaning does your baby's name hold?

   ....

   ....

   ....

   ....

3. What were some other names you considered for your baby?

   ....

   ....

   ....

   ....

4. Our baby's name is a family name. The other family member(s) who shares our baby's name has these special characteristics:

   ....

   ....

   ....

   ....

5. What was particularly challenging about deciding on a name, and what methods did you use to narrow down the options?

   ....

   ....

   ....

   ....

Display a birth certificate.

Born on the 4th of July BY KIM KESTI

Tip: I wanted to use my mother's birth certificate on this layout since the focus is the actual date of her birth. I scanned it and printed the document quite a bit smaller to allow it to fit easily on my layout.

—*Kim Kesti*

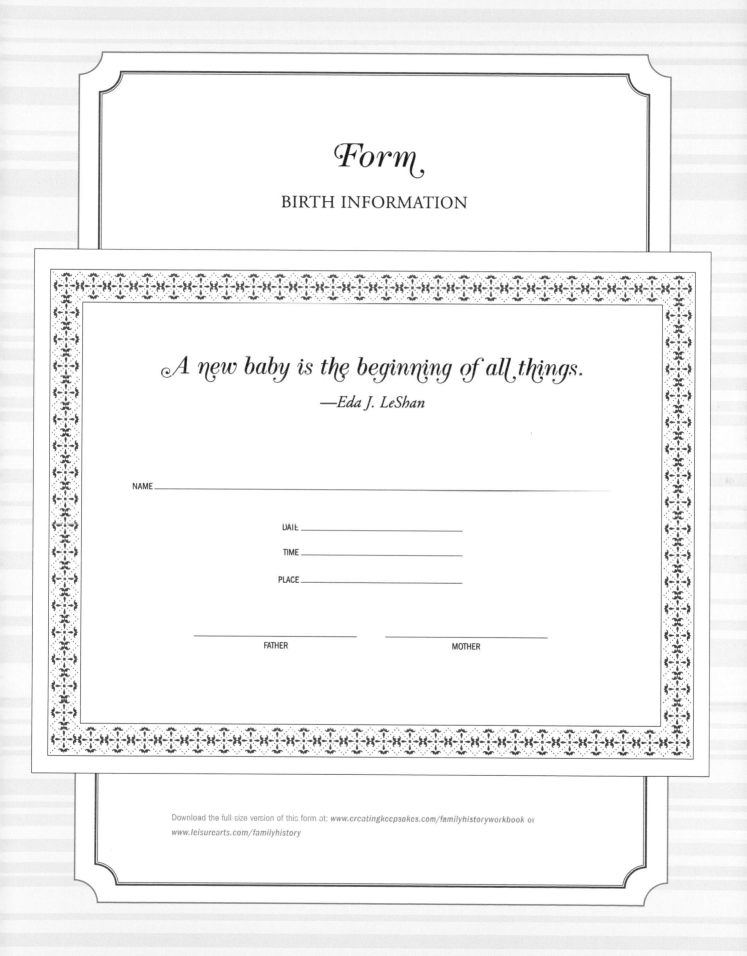

Form

BIRTH INFORMATION

A new baby is the beginning of all things.

—Eda J. LeShan

NAME _____

DATE _____

TIME _____

PLACE _____

_____   _____
FATHER   MOTHER

Download the full-size version of this form at: *www.creatingkeepsakes.com/familyhistoryworkbook* or *www.leisurearts.com/familyhistory*

Celebrate a first birthday.

to: Kay

xoxo:

3.31.50

So My mom looks sweet here on her 1st birthday. This is one of the only photos we have recording a birthday because Mom says she never really had birthday parties.

Kay's First Birthday BY SHELLEY LAMING

Tip: It's okay to record the sadder side of things. My mom looks back on never really having had birthday parties, not with pity but with the outlook that that was just the way things were. —*Shelley Laming*

Worksheet

FIRST BIRTHDAY

1. What special plans did you make for your child's first birthday?

   ....
   ....
   ....

2. What family members or friends were involved in this special day?

   ....
   ....
   ....

3. What skills and abilities did your child have by his or her first birthday?

   ....
   ....
   ....

4. What was your child's favorite part of the day?

   ....
   ....
   ....

5. What special memories do you have from the first year of your child's life?

   ....
   ....
   ....

Scrapbook a baptism story.

one Lord
one Faith
one Baptism
Mary Louise
1930

Louise's Baptism BY SHELLEY LAMING

Tip: Using a variety of pastel colors and patterns easily evokes the "baby" feel. This photo has a heavy sepia tone, but that doesn't mean you have to scrapbook it using dark and dreary colors. —*Shelley Laming*

Worksheet

OUR BLESSED BABY

1. What location did you select for the baby blessing? Why?

   ....

   ....

   ....

   ....

2. What special messages were a part of the baby's blessing?

   ....

   ....

   ....

   ....

3. Who attended the blessing?

   ....

   ....

   ....

4. Did your baby wear a special outfit for the blessing? What significance does it have?

   ....

   ....

   ....

   ....

5. What was the most memorable part of the day?

   ....

   ....

   ....

Tell a baby story.

Dwight Julin Larson
Summer 1942

Baby
BOY

This is my favorite photo of my dad as a baby. It sat on my grandmother's desk in her home until she passed away. I remember being fascinated by it when I was a child. I love that my dad looks very much the same now as he did when he was a baby. I love how his grandfather, Lewis Dwight Trumbull is looking down at him. It's so endearing how Grandpa Trumbull put his hat on Dad. I love that they are in Maiden Rock, Wisconsin on the grounds of the home where my grandmother grew up. I will always treasure having this photo.

Baby Boy BY VICKI HARVEY

Worksheet

A BABY STORY

1. What physical attributes did you notice about your baby?
   Did he or she resemble any family members?

   ....
   ....
   ....
   ....

2. What special endearing characteristics are unique to your baby?

   ....
   ....
   ....
   ....

3. What family circumstances and dynamics was your baby
   born in to?

   ....
   ....
   ....
   ....

4. Share a funny or memorable story unique to your child.

   ....
   ....
   ....
   ....

5. What special thing did you do that your baby always loved?

   ....
   ....
   ....
   ....

Record a baby's first moments.

NAME Lelynn Trumbull

from the back of the photo:

"with my sister Lucile on Grandma Julin's farm. Taken before September 1910 My first picture."

- Uncle Lelynn and Grandma

1st Photo BY VICKI HARVEY

Tip: Make sure you check the back of your photographs for any identifying information. Use that information for your journaling. —*Vicki Harvey*

Worksheet

BABY'S FIRSTS

List the date and explain a few details about the following firsts in a baby's life:

1. First smile

_____

_____

_____

2. First tooth

_____

_____

_____

3. First real food

_____

_____

_____

4. First word

_____

_____

_____

5. First injury

_____

_____

_____

Share a "welcome home" story.

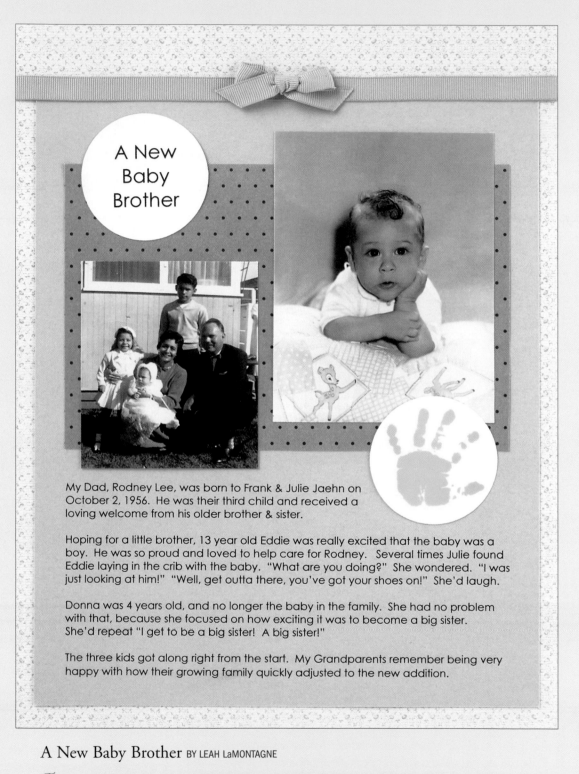

A New Baby Brother

My Dad, Rodney Lee, was born to Frank & Julie Jaehn on October 2, 1956. He was their third child and received a loving welcome from his older brother & sister.

Hoping for a little brother, 13 year old Eddie was really excited that the baby was a boy. He was so proud and loved to help care for Rodney. Several times Julie found Eddie laying in the crib with the baby. "What are you doing?" She wondered. "I was just looking at him!" "Well, get outta there, you've got your shoes on!" She'd laugh.

Donna was 4 years old, and no longer the baby in the family. She had no problem with that, because she focused on how exciting it was to become a big sister. She'd repeat "I get to be a big sister! A big sister!"

The three kids got along right from the start. My Grandparents remember being very happy with how their growing family quickly adjusted to the new addition.

A New Baby Brother BY LEAH LaMONTAGNE

Tip: It can be difficult for family members to remember the details of a baby's birth from a while back. Asking very specific questions can get a memory going and ignite an understanding of exactly what type of information you're seeking. —*Leah LaMontagne*

Worksheet

BABY ARRIVAL STORY

1. How did your family respond to the new baby's arrival?

2. Did one member of your family have a particularly hard time adjusting to the change?

3. What types of things did you do to make the transition easier?

4. What was an unexpected but pleasant surprise during this transition period?

5. What did you learn about your family during this time?

Tell a grandparent's story.

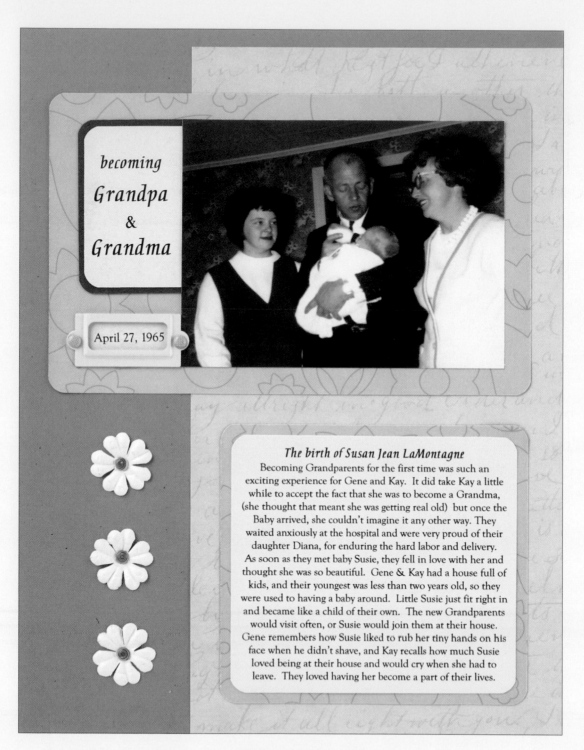

becoming Grandpa & Grandma

April 27, 1965

The birth of Susan Jean LaMontagne

Becoming Grandparents for the first time was such an exciting experience for Gene and Kay. It did take Kay a little while to accept the fact that she was to become a Grandma, (she thought that meant she was getting real old) but once the Baby arrived, she couldn't imagine it any other way. They waited anxiously at the hospital and were very proud of their daughter Diana, for enduring the hard labor and delivery. As soon as they met baby Susie, they fell in love with her and thought she was so beautiful. Gene & Kay had a house full of kids, and their youngest was less than two years old, so they were used to having a baby around. Little Susie just fit right in and became like a child of their own. The new Grandparents would visit often, or Susie would join them at their house. Gene remembers how Susie liked to rub her tiny hands on his face when he didn't shave, and Kay recalls how much Susie loved being at their house and would cry when she had to leave. They loved having her become a part of their lives.

Becoming Grandpa & Grandma BY LEAH LaMONTAGNE

Worksheet

BECOMING A GRANDPARENT

1. When did you first become a grandparent and to whom?
   What were the events surrounding the birth?

   ....

   ....

   ....

   ....

2. How did you feel about your new role?

   ....

   ....

   ....

   ....

3. What attributes did you notice about your new grandchild?
   Did he or she look like any other members of the family?

   ....

   ....

   ....

   ....

4. What other grandchildren do you have, and when were they born?

   ....

   ....

   ....

   ....

5. In what ways did you change after becoming a grandparent?

   ....

   ....

   ....

   ....

Page Planner 5

Use the page planner on the opposite page as a starting point for creating your own scrapbook pages. Here's how Carey used the page planner to tell a favorite family story.

Hang on and Hold

When I was on bedrest with Beckett, my aunt sent me an E-mail telling me about my great-grandma Christina's first pregnancy. She was living in the country at the time, and she suddenly had major pain in her stomach. She thought that she was losing her baby. She had to ride in the back of a bouncing truck into town; she was very sick and I am sure began to worry about her own health, but I know how helpless she must have felt, not being able to control your own body. It ended up being appendicitis, and she was very very ill, but she ended up delivering her first born, my grandpa Gibby, in 1916. (Above, infant 1916, at one 1917 and at two in 1918.) I am so lucky to have known grandpa and Grandma Tina.

Hang On BY CAREY JOHNSON

Tip: Scan old photos and then crop them digitally to show detail. —*Carey Johnson*

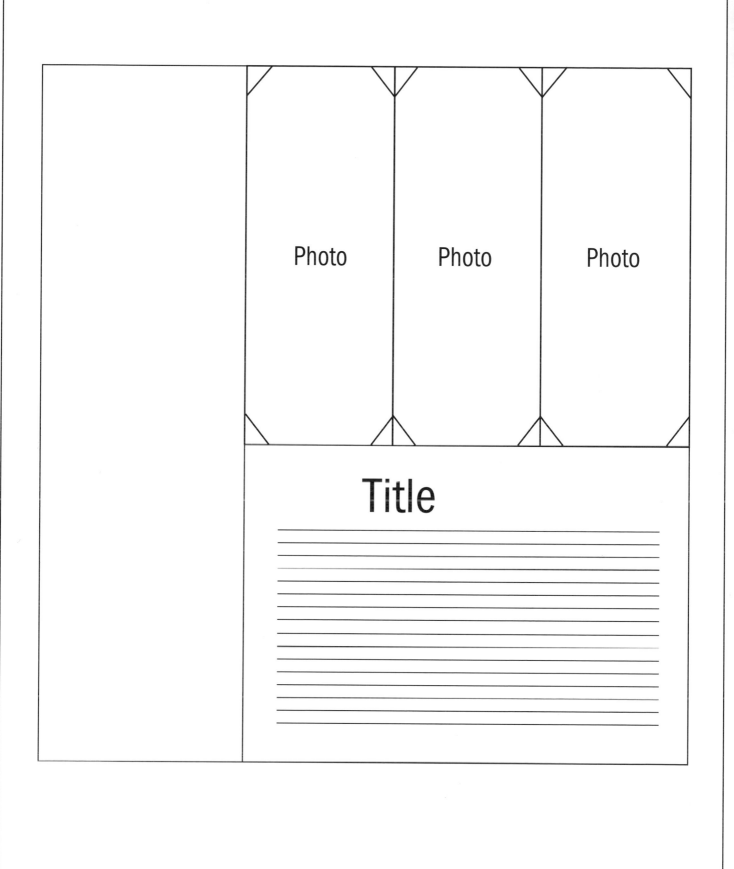

Photo

Photo

Photo

Title

Page Planner 6

Use the page planner on the opposite page as a starting point for creating your own scrapbook pages. Here's how Carey used the page planner to tell a favorite family story.

My mom, like me, smiles all the time. She is known for her beautiful and genuine smile. She ALWAYS has her lipstick perfectly applied and it doesn't take much for her to laugh. So, when I found these photos of her as a little girl, they made ME smile. She looks so somber. Geesh, lighten up a little mom!

1948 & 1949

Mary Moldestad-Hartmann

Be Mary BY CAREY JOHNSON

Tip: I cut the birds out of the paper to add a more whimsical look and used a fine-point marker to add the legs. I didn't have much information about these photographs, so I designed the page to reflect my mom's current personality. —*Carey Johnson*

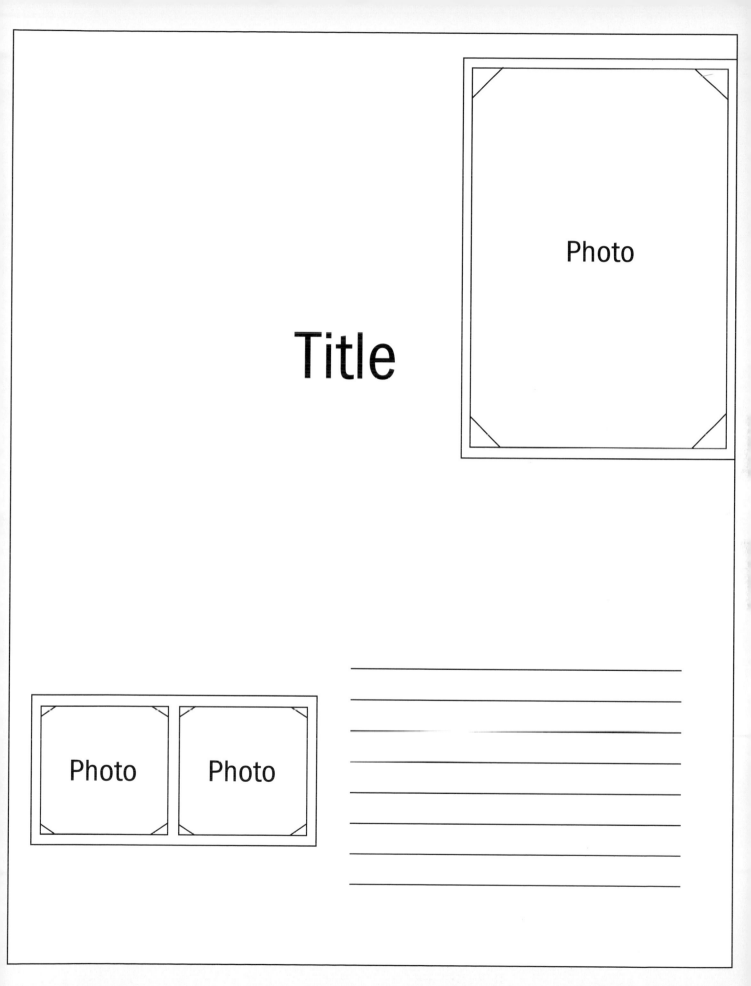

Photo

Title

Photo   Photo

Family Album
Q&A with Shelley Laming

Everyday Moments   BY SHELLEY LAMING

Why did you decide to create this album?

In addition to having a bigger heritage album, I thought it would be nice to have a small album containing special photos that didn't necessarily have a story or event behind them. I wanted to capture and celebrate the "everyday" moments.

Why is this album important to you?

It's important to me because it shows a more candid side of life.

Is this a stand-alone album or part of a series?

I would like to have more than one album like this—so if I find more photos that fit, I'll keep going after filling this album.

I adore this photo of Louise and Maurice from about 1938. Lu is sharing her dollies with her little brother. He looks like a doll himself!

sharing

How long did your project take?

It took me about three or four hours to complete the album.

They say grandparents "back then" were a lot of times more gruff than loving. But this photo of my great-grandma and Lu clearly shows she was of the loving variety.

loving

Rosa Azaline Coulter w/Lu c. 1930

5

What's your best advice on family history scrapbooking?

Picking a theme (I chose verbs, like loving, laughing, playing) helps a mini album come together very easily. Keep it simple and in a style you love. Don't get caught up with re-creating current scrapbook trends, because you want your album to be something you love looking at for years to come.

chapter 4

Childhood/ Teen Years

"Our whole life is but a greater and longer childhood."
— Benjamin Franklin

There may have been others, but this ninth birthday party was the first one Nana Mary (my mom) remembers as having actually been a "real" party, complete with invited friends beyond just family. The twins, Richard and Mary, turned nine on January 8, 1959 and celebrated at their Parker, WA home. Nana Mary clearly recalls the two cakes their stepmom made for them...a white doll cake (where the cake was the skirt of the doll and an actual doll stuck out of the top) for her and a chocolate train cake for her brother. As usual (given the Filipino culture), there was plenty of food, but Nana Mary remembers most fondly the fact that it was an official party.

First REAL Party

First Real Party BY AMANDA PROBST

Worksheet

A CHILDHOOD FIRST

1. What was a first for you that was significant in your young life?

_____

_____

_____

2. Why was it particularly important or meaningful?

_____

_____

_____

3. Were there any family members or friends involved in this milestone? If so, who?

_____

_____

_____

4. What are some of your fondest memories of that time?

_____

_____

_____

5. What do your parents have to say about that time in your life?

_____

_____

_____

Share a story about a childhood favorite.

This is one of Nana Mary's favorite pictures from her

childhood…and is incidentally of one of her favorite

memories. Though the family didn't

have much in the way of

material wealth, the holidays were

a special time for gathering with

family, eating lots of food and

simply being together. Being five

years apart, Nana Mary and her big

sister Delores didn't have much

in common. At Christmas, though,

the two were jointly in charge of

decorating the tree and Nana Mary

treasured those moments. *Mary & Delores 12/1958*

FAVORITE TIME OF YEAR

Favorite Time of Year BY AMANDA PROBST

Worksheet

A CHILDHOOD FAVORITE

Fill in a few details about these childhood favorites:

1. Favorite toys/friend

....
....
....
....

2. Favorite words

....
....
....
....

3. Favorite music or song

....
....
....
....

4. Favorite food

....
....
....
....

5. Favorite activities

....
....
....

Journal about school days.

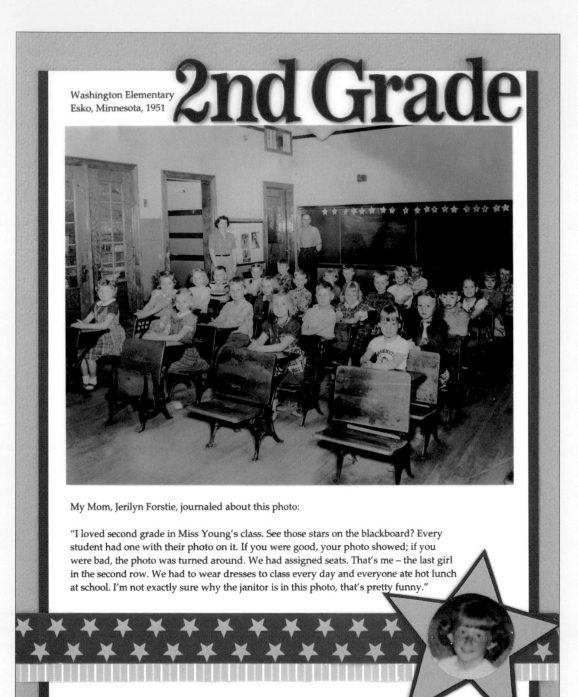

Washington Elementary
Esko, Minnesota, 1951

2nd Grade

My Mom, Jerilyn Forstie, journaled about this photo:

"I loved second grade in Miss Young's class. See those stars on the blackboard? Every student had one with their photo on it. If you were good, your photo showed; if you were bad, the photo was turned around. We had assigned seats. That's me – the last girl in the second row. We had to wear dresses to class every day and everyone ate hot lunch at school. I'm not exactly sure why the janitor is in this photo, that's pretty funny."

2nd Grade BY KIM KESTI

Tip: I used primary colors on this layout to reinforce the school theme. I wanted to play up the story of the stars on the blackboard, so I created my own star accent by framing a small photo of my mother.

—*Kim Kesti*

Worksheet

SCHOOL DAYS

1. What is the name and location of the first school you attended?

----

2. What was your favorite teacher's name, and what memories do you have of him or her?

----

3. What memories do you have about your first day of school?

----

4. How did you get to and from school?

----

5. What were your feelings about school as a child? What did you like or dislike?

Share an extracurricular experience.

Band Geek BY KIM KESTI

Tip: Don't be afraid to use heritage photographs in conjunction with today's vocabulary! It can add an extra layer of meaning to your pages. —*Kim Kesti*

Worksheet

ACTIVITIES

1. What was your favorite sport or activity, and what was your level of involvement throughout your childhood/teenage years?

   _____

   _____

   _____

   _____

2. At what age did you begin playing or following the sport?

   _____

   _____

   _____

   _____

3. What other sports/activities interested you?

   _____

   _____

   _____

   _____

4. Talk about some memorable incidents that took place during a sporting event or activity.

   _____

   _____

   _____

   _____

5. What were and are your favorite things about this sport or activity?

   _____

   _____

   _____

   _____

Celebrate young friendships.

Linda, Sharon, and Kay
circa 1952

Not just sisters...
but best friends.

Through thick and thin,
through out life...

always close.

Linda, Sharon and Kay BY SHELLEY LAMING

Worksheet

BEST FRIENDS

1. What is the name of your childhood best friend? At what age did you become friends? How did you meet?

   ....

   ....

   ....

2. What other friends did you have at this time?

   ....

   ....

   ....

3. What were some of your favorite activities to do together?

   ....

   ....

   ....

4. What dispute did you have that impacted your friendship? How was it resolved, and how did it change your relationship?

   ....

   ....

   ....

5. What characteristics did you admire about your friend? Are you still in contact with him or her?

   ....

   ....

   ....

Recall a favorite childhood trip.

charmed

Abbyville, La.-1959

When my mom (on the right in top photo) went to Abbyville for Maurice's wedding, she remembers being impressed by everyone's southern charm. This trip to the "city" was a big deal to her because vacations were few and far between. She remembers Aunt Dot as a truly gracious person who made her feel special.

Charmed BY SHELLEY LAMING

Tip: A good way to ground two photos is to mat them on the same piece of cardstock to create one large photo mat. —*Shelley Laming*

Worksheet

A FAVORITE VACATION

1. Share the details of your most memorable childhood vacation.

   ....

   ....

   ....

2. Did your family go on an annual vacation to the same location? What are some of your memories surrounding that tradition?

   ....

   ....

   ....

3. Describe a family vacation that ended in disaster or mishap. How did your family members respond?

   ....

   ....

   ....

4. What made a particular family vacation special?

   ....

   ....

   ....

5. What type of transportation did your family use to get to the destination? What type of activities did your family do to pass the traveling time?

   ....

   ....

   ....

The Obligatory Christmas Photo BY VICKI HARVEY

Tip: Use several photos from the same decade to showcase a specific subject. Use unconventional colors for a fun look. —*Vicki Harvey*

Worksheet

A MEMORABLE HOLIDAY

1. What was your favorite childhood holiday? Why?

   ....

   ....

   ....

2. What family traditions surrounded the holiday?

   ....

   ....

   ....

3. What family members attended family gatherings or celebrations? Include memories about each individual.

   ....

   ....

   ....

4. What is a funny memory you have of a holiday celebration?

   ....

   ....

   ....

5. What are some favorite smells or foods associated with holiday celebrations?

   ....

   ....

   ....

Within the layout:
It's so fun seeing the goofy side of my parents when they were teenagers. This first love ultimately turned into marriage.

Dwight + Ruthie circa 1962

FUN

first love

First Love BY VICKI HARVEY

Tip: Even if a couple is no longer married, there's a story behind the beginning of their relationship. Talk to them to find out about it. —*Vicki Harvey*

Worksheet

YOUNG LOVE

1. Share the details of your first crush.

_____

_____

_____

2. What embarrassing or funny memory do you have of a date?

_____

_____

_____

3. What friends and associations did you make during the
   dating years?

_____

_____

_____

4. What individual did you most enjoy dating?

_____

_____

_____

5. What was your first date like?

_____

_____

_____

Share a favorite childhood memory.

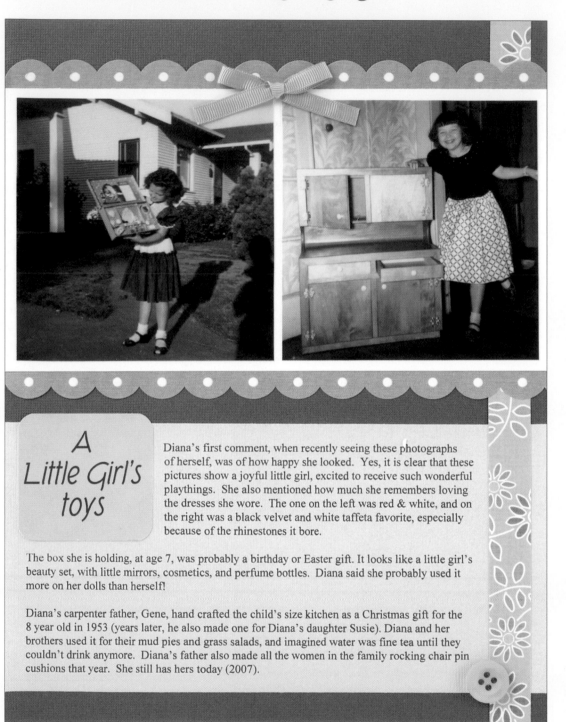

A Little Girl's toys

Diana's first comment, when recently seeing these photographs of herself, was of how happy she looked. Yes, it is clear that these pictures show a joyful little girl, excited to receive such wonderful playthings. She also mentioned how much she remembers loving the dresses she wore. The one on the left was red & white, and on the right was a black velvet and white taffeta favorite, especially because of the rhinestones it bore.

The box she is holding, at age 7, was probably a birthday or Easter gift. It looks like a little girl's beauty set, with little mirrors, cosmetics, and perfume bottles. Diana said she probably used it more on her dolls than herself!

Diana's carpenter father, Gene, hand crafted the child's size kitchen as a Christmas gift for the 8 year old in 1953 (years later, he also made one for Diana's daughter Susie). Diana and her brothers used it for their mud pies and grass salads, and imagined water was fine tea until they couldn't drink anymore. Diana's father also made all the women in the family rocking chair pin cushions that year. She still has hers today (2007).

A Little Girl's Toys BY LEAH LaMONTAGNE

Tip: Black-and-white photos are easy to scrapbook because you don't have to worry about choosing colors that will complement the photos. You can, however, choose colors and patterns that will emphasize the story you're trying to portray. —*Leah LaMontagne*

Worksheet

A CHILDHOOD MEMORY

1. Describe the details of a favorite childhood memory.

   ....

   ....

   ....

   ....

2. What individuals were involved in the event or occurrence?

   ....

   ....

   ....

   ....

3. Why is the memory so meaningful?

   ....

   ....

   ....

   ....

4. What details about the memory do you wish you knew more about?

   ....

   ....

   ....

   ....

5. Create a list of questions you can ask other family members or associations to add more details or facts to the story.

   ....

   ....

   ....

   ....

Journal about your childhood home.

Home Sweet Home
in the 1930's

812 8th Street, Rapid City, South Dakota: My Grandpa's final childhood home. His family moved into the house when he was about 15 years old. He lived there until he graduated from high school in 1939 and moved to California. Frank Jr., my Grandfather, shared a big bedroom with his 7 siblings. His parents, Frank Sr. and Madeline Jaehn rented the home for about $35 per month. It was on a main road that lead right up to Mount Rushmore (22 miles away) and it was half a block from down town's Main Street. When a parade was held, they could watch it right from their porch as it came from Main Street and down their road. The porch was a favorite place to relax and socialize in the summertime.

During the winter, the home was heated by the basement coal furnace. The winter snowfall was fierce, and Frank remembers walking to school in waist high snow. They had a big garden in their front yard, right between the sidewalk and the street. Although it was a busy road, no one ever bothered the garden. They grew many different types of vegetables. The kids would help water and weed, and Madeline would cook or can the vegetables. The pictures here show Frank Sr. using a cultivator with his sons (my Grandpa's brothers) Leonard, Gene, and Milo. Their neighborhood hangout was Mill's drug store, where there was a Soda Fountain and they could enjoy treats like ice cream floats, Coca Cola, and candy or popcorn. My Grandpa remembers a church and funeral home across the street. Relatives from his Mother's side would often visit, and they would celebrate Holidays together at home.

Home Sweet Home BY LEAH LaMONTAGNE

Worksheet

MY HOME

1. What is your earliest or fondest memory of home?

_____

_____

_____

_____

2. What was your favorite thing about your childhood home?

_____

_____

_____

_____

3. What was your room like in your family home?

_____

_____

_____

_____

4. What ages were you when you lived in your childhood home? How many homes did you live in while you were growing up?

_____

_____

_____

_____

5. What condition is the home in today? Do you know the owner?

_____

_____

_____

_____

Page Planner 7

Use the page planner on the opposite page as a starting point for creating your own scrapbook pages. Here's how Carey used the page planner to tell a favorite family story.

One thing I notice when I look through all of the countless photos of my dad's childhood is the abundance of photos of him, and his siblings, doing activities. I know my dad loved his train set and played with his erector set a lot, and I know he played the trumpet all the way through college. I didn't know he was such a little dancer, but I learned something new from these photos (although I have a feeling his sister had something to do with the above photo.) I also know that as a child, there were still many of his games and toys at my grandparent's house. I used to love to look at those and even play with them from time to time. It seems like my dad and his siblings were pretty active kids.

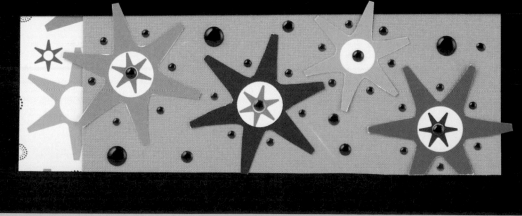

Play BY CAREY JOHNSON

Tip: Remember to tell stories about how your family plays together. —*Carey Johnson*

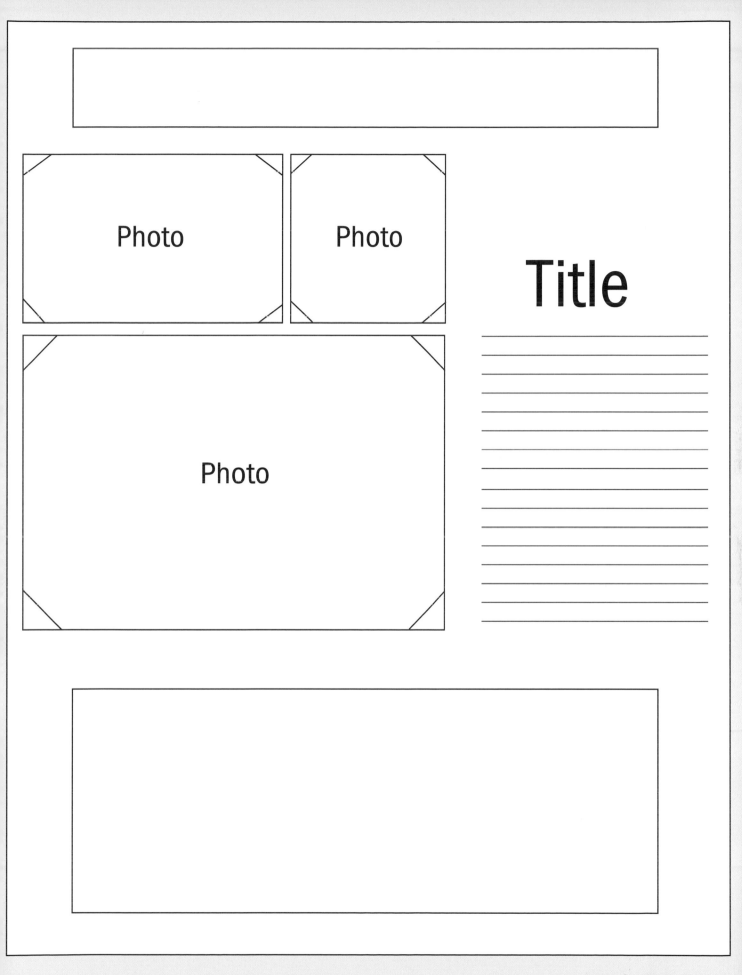

Photo

Photo

Title

Use the page planner on the opposite page as a starting point for creating your own scrapbook pages. Here's how Carey used the page planner to tell a favorite family story.

Paula BY CAREY JOHNSON

Tip: I printed my title directly on the patterned paper to give it emphasis and texture. I also used my computer to create journaling that wraps around the title and photos. —*Carey Johnson*

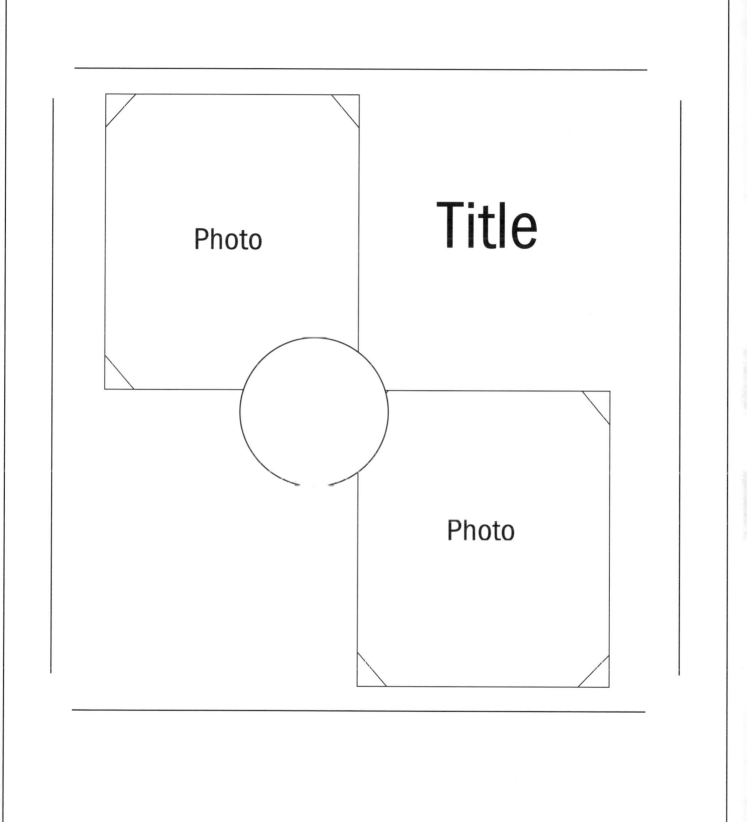

Title

Photo

Photo

Family Album
Q&A with Vicki Harvey

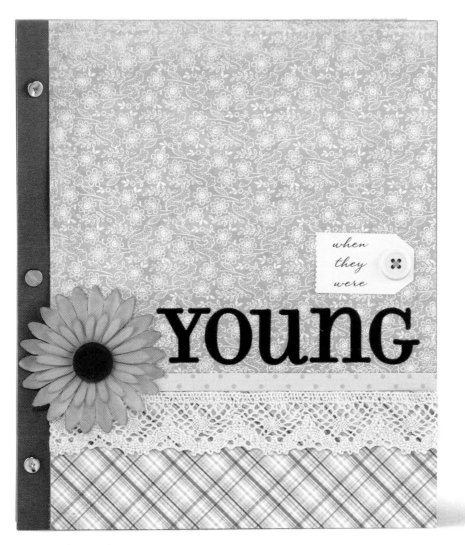

When They Were Young BY VICKI HARVEY

Why did you decide to create this album?

I'm amazed at all of the changes in the world, even since I was younger. I thought it would be interesting for my children to hear what life was like for the generations that came before them.

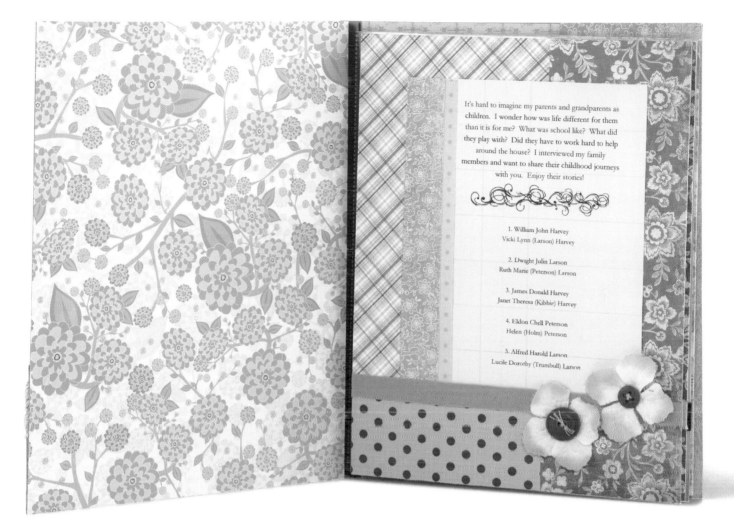

Why is this album important to you?

I had an incredible experience speaking with my grandparents and my parents about their childhoods. My grandfather was smiling and laughing as he remembered the toys he had and things he had done. My dad initially told me there was no way he could remember those years. By the time I finished my album, he had called me about seven times to relate different stories he had remembered. He told me I had jogged his memory back to that time. It was a great connection for me.

Dwight Julin Larson

born 9-16-41

My dad was raised in town. He would come home from school and his mom would be there cooking dinner for the family. He played outside a lot. In the winter he and his friends would go to the sledding hill or the skating rink to play hockey. Once, and only once, he put his tongue on the playground equipment at school! In the summer he played kickball. He had only one bike during these years. It was ironically purchased from his future father-in-law. Once in awhile he and his friends would go and play at a nearby farm. That was special since he lived in town and didn't get to play in the barns everyday. He didn't have a lot of chores to do - just to take the newspaper out and burn it in the burn barrel. At home he didn't play with his sister Nita very much. She was five years older than he was. He enjoyed playing with an erector set he received one Christmas. That was a special gift. When he was in high school he was quite shy. He didn't date or go to dances. He went out for football, baseball and basketball and enjoyed that. He worked two summers at the Green Giant canning factory in town and made 95 cents an hour!

Ruth Marie (Peterson) Larson

born 7-12-46

My mom was raised on a farm. She and her brother, Duane, played outside a lot. When they got home from school they would change clothes (they weren't allowed to play in their school clothes) and go outside. In the winter they would go sledding and have snowball fights. When the weather was warm they would play in the barn, play with the dogs or play ball. They didn't have a lot of toys. She had a doll, but she didn't like it very much. She liked playing games like Monopoly or card games like Snap, Go Fish and Rummy better. She and Duane were expected to do the dishes every evening after supper. Sometimes they would do more fighting than dish washing. She disliked doing dishes on Mondays in particular because that was baking day and there were a lot more pans and bowls to wash. Once she was in junior high school her responsibilities increased as her mother went to work at the local grocery store. She was expected to cook supper every evening and clean the house on Saturday mornings.

Is this a stand-alone album or part of a series?

At this point, it's a stand-alone album. It could be a series, however, featuring the same people but with each album telling the story about different times in their lives.

How long did your project take?

It took me 6–8 hours to complete this project.

Eldon Chell Peterson

born 2-15-21

My grandfather was born and raised on a farm. He was the only boy in a family of four children. He went to French Lake Country School until the eighth grade. After school he would come home and do his chores and then play by himself. He didn't have any neighbors close enough to play with him. He had a few toys. He played with a Fordson cast iron tractor for many years. He wore out a little truck made of steel from using it so much! He also remembers an airplane that hung from the ceiling by a string. It went spinning around in circles when it was wound up. When he was twelve he got a tricycle as a gift. One day his mother found him in the barn with the tricycle in pieces all around him. When she asked him what on earth he was doing, he said he was taking it apart to see how it worked! He still has that mechanical mind to this day. His after school chores included bringing wood and water into the house since there was no running water or electricity. When he was about 14 years old he had to help out with the farm chores. He would only go to school in the winter months because his help was needed with planting and harvesting.

Helen Florence (Holm) Peterson

born 5-30-29

My grandmother was born and raised in Cokato, Minnesota, a small farming town west of the Twin Cities. She was the oldest of eight children. When she grew up there was no electricity or running water. There was no television to keep them occupied. She attended a one room country school called Beaver Dam School. Eight grades were in the one room. After school she would come home to do chores like carrying in water and wood. She helped with the cooking and baking. She also helped out with her siblings since her mother worked at Johnson Produce and her father worked at Northland Canning Company. She didn't have many toys. They were not a wealthy family. Some years there were only Christmas gifts from friends because there was no money for the family to buy gifts. She made up games to play - counting the cars along the road or counting the box cars on the trains. Hide & seek and tag were also favorite outdoor games. She had a few board games like checkers and playing cards. When she played Old Maid there wasn't a special deck. One of the queens was just left in as the Old Maid card.

What's your best advice on family history scrapbooking?

Interview your family members now. My paternal grandmother has passed away, and I would give anything to interview her about her childhood. I think the stories would be so interesting.

chapter 5

Adult Years

"Old age is like climbing a mountain. You climb from ledge to ledge. The higher you get, the more tired and breathless you become, but your views become more extensive."
— *Ingrid Bergman*

Your dad's Grandpa Al's first real job was with radio station KPQ in Wenatchee, WA. He was an apprentice, and started out as a jack of all trades (including janitorial work)...advancing to salesman, copy writer and eventually news broadcaster. This was in 1936 after graduating from Wenatchee High School.

In 1941, Grandpa Al says he'd just gotten out of church on Sunday morning when he heard about the Japanese attack on Pearl Harbor. Knowing he would be drafted, he decided if he were to serve he'd prefer the Navy. He went to San Diego for boot training "not knowing diddly" as he put it. After various aptitude tests, Grandpa Al was sent to the University of Houston for further training then transferred to Corpus Christi, TX after four months. He then moved to Navy Air Station (Ward Island), having been transferred to the air division of the Navy. He did a lot of flying, inspecting the radar installation, identifying equipment and either approving or denying its workability. His last move was in the service was to MIT in Boston, MA. He married Grandma Helen in Providence, RI in July of 1945 and, having fulfilled his service contract, returned to Boston to receive his discharge papers. Papers in hand, he bought a 1939 DeSota and headed for home (WA). He says he had to buy all new tires on the way home, as the ones on the car weren't good and had to be replaced one at a time.

Grandpa Al & Grandma Helen have lived in the Yakima, WA area for the remainder of their marriage (and do so today), where Grandpa Al used to work in the music business, owning and operating an organ store.

spring 1942 – Al, bootcamp

Navy BY AMANDA PROBST

Worksheet

WORKING FOR A LIVING

1. What was your first job, your title and place of employment? How long did you hold the position?

_____
_____
_____
_____

2. What were your job duties?

_____
_____
_____
_____

3. How did you feel about your first job?

_____
_____
_____
_____

4. What was your boss like? What characteristics did you like or dislike about him or her?

_____
_____
_____
_____

5. What life lessons did you learn from your first job?

_____
_____
_____

SMITH *Family* HOME

My Grandpa (Steve) Smith and his brother Jack built this house on Horse Heaven hills in Prosser, WA so that Steve would have a home to bring his bride to. His bride, Ann Cvar, lived in East Helena, MT as did most of Grandpa's relatives. (Steve, his parents and family had come to Prosser in 1918, leaving the rest of the family in East Helena.) Steve had been living in a little shack on the grounds prior to this house being built. The shack was later relocated to Jack's land nearby.

Once settled in their new house after being married in East Helena in November 1938, Steve and Ann set about filling it. The couple had 8 living children. The four boys shared the basement and the four girls shared the front two bedrooms. Originally, the house was white, but in the 1950s Steve got some sort of deal with a siding salesman (according to my dad, Robert) and added green siding, which is how your Papa Robert always remembers the home. In the late 1960s or early 1970s, the siding was changed to yellow.

After all of the Smith kids had left home and Grandpa (Steve) had died, the brothers and sisters retained joint ownership of the property as part of the family corporation (Kovach Land Company). Over the years, various family members have stayed there, family gatherings have taken place there and for a time it was rented out. I, personally, remember many a Thanksgiving spent in that house, mostly avoiding the basement for fear of rats… playing touch football in the field and hide and seek amid the farm buildings and chicken coop. Currently, it stands vacant but remains the heart of the Smith family farm.

photo taken 1990s

Smith Family Home BY AMANDA PROBST

Worksheet

A FIRST HOME

1. Where was your first home? What is the exact address?

   ....

   ....

   ....

   ....

2. Talk about some of the details of your home (new or existing, square footage, style, number of bedrooms, exterior/interior colors, odd details, etc.).

   ....

   ....

   ....

   ....

3. How much did you pay for your first home?

   ....

   ....

   ....

   ....

4. What did you like most about your first home, or what sold you on buying it?

   ....

   ....

   ....

   ....

5. How big was your family when you moved into your first home?

   ....

   ....

   ....

   ....

Journal about dating or courtship.

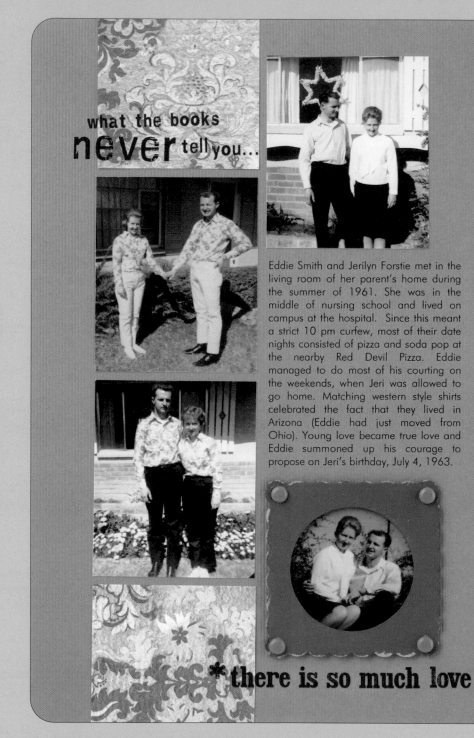

what the books **never** tell you...

Eddie Smith and Jerilyn Forstie met in the living room of her parent's home during the summer of 1961. She was in the middle of nursing school and lived on campus at the hospital. Since this meant a strict 10 pm curfew, most of their date nights consisted of pizza and soda pop at the nearby Red Devil Pizza. Eddie managed to do most of his courting on the weekends, when Jeri was allowed to go home. Matching western style shirts celebrated the fact that they lived in Arizona (Eddie had just moved from Ohio). Young love became true love and Eddie summoned up his courage to propose on Jeri's birthday, July 4, 1963.

*there is so much love

What the Books Never Tell You BY KIM KESTI

Tip: Since my parents' courtship took place in the sixties, I used colors on my layout to reflect that era. I also left the photos in their original colors even though some of them were slightly faded. —*Kim Kesti*

Worksheet

DATING

1. How did you meet your significant other? What first impressions did you have of each other?

_____

_____

_____

2. What was your first date like? What made you decide to continue dating each other?

_____

_____

_____

3. What were some notable world or community events that took place during your courtship? How did they impact your relationship?

_____

_____

_____

4. What types of things did you enjoy doing as you got to know each other?

_____

_____

_____

5. What differences or similarities did you notice as you became more acquainted with each other?

_____

_____

_____

Recall an engagement.

I'll love you **forever**

-matching shirts

-matching shorts

-matching futures

Ken and Edna were engaged just before the wedding of a mutual friend. Edna was attending Wayne State University in Detroit and Ken worked for General Motors for $5.00 an hour. Life couldn't be better.

October 1962

Matching Futures BY KIM KESTI

Tip: Sometimes, less is more. I felt like this photo really tells the story of Ken and Edna, so I left the layout simple, with three bullet points to support the title. —*Kim Kesti*

Worksheet

THE ENGAGEMENT

1. Tell the story of your marriage proposal.

_____

_____

_____

_____

2. How did you feel about this special time? Were you expecting the proposal to take place?

_____

_____

_____

_____

3. What disagreements did you have during your engagement? How did they impact your relationship?

_____

_____

_____

_____

4. Describe your rings and why they were chosen.

_____

_____

_____

_____

5. In what ways did you grow closer during your engagement?

_____

_____

_____

_____

SEEING THIS PHOTO FROM MY GRANDPARENTS' WEDDING DAY ALWAYS MAKES ME SMILE. THEIR EXPRESSIONS SAY IT ALL... I SEE SUCH LOVE THERE. THIS DAY MARKED THE START OF A BEAUTIFUL LIFE TOGETHER.

William Jackson Abercrombie

♥

Chellie Irene Coulter

12.24.28

12.24.28 BY SHELLEY LAMING

Worksheet

THE WEDDING

1. What location did you choose for your wedding and why? Does it have special significance?

....

....

....

2. What special advice or comments were given by the wedding officiator?

....

....

....

3. What guests attended your wedding?

....

....

....

4. Describe any glitches or bumps that occurred on your wedding day.

....

....

....

5. What is one memory of your wedding day that you will always remember?

....

....

....

Share a difficult experience.

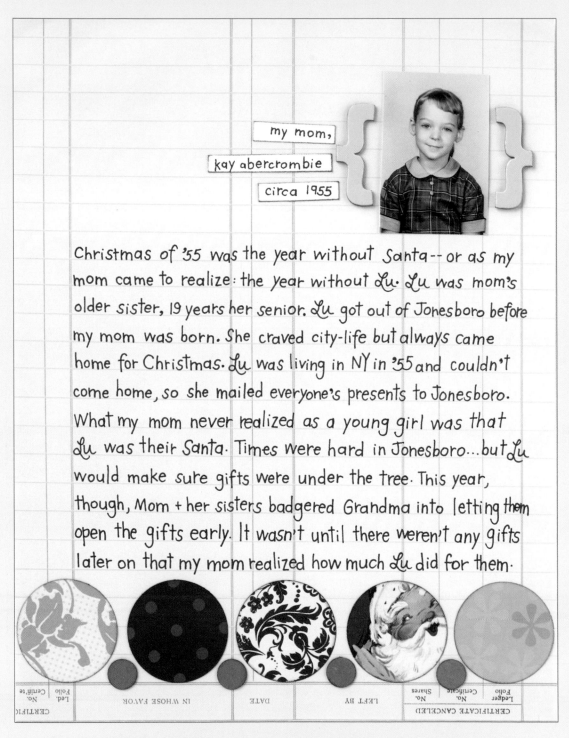

my mom,

kay abercrombie

circa 1955

Christmas of '55 was the year without Santa-- or as my mom came to realize: the year without Lu. Lu was mom's older sister, 19 years her senior. Lu got out of Jonesboro before my mom was born. She craved city-life but always came home for Christmas. Lu was living in NY in '55 and couldn't come home, so she mailed everyone's presents to Jonesboro. What my mom never realized as a young girl was that Lu was their Santa. Times were hard in Jonesboro...but Lu would make sure gifts were under the tree. This year, though, Mom + her sisters badgered Grandma into letting them open the gifts early. It wasn't until there weren't any gifts later on that my mom realized how much Lu did for them.

Christmas '55 BY SHELLEY LAMING

Tip: Using vintage graphics is an easy way to add something special to a page. Also, if you don't have a photo that specifically illustrates the story you want to tell, just find a photo from the same time period.

—*Shelley Laming*

Worksheet

TOUGH TIMES

1. Describe the details of a difficult time in your life.

....

....

....

....

2. What made this time so challenging? How did you cope
   with it?

....

....

....

....

3. What did you learn about yourself that you didn't know
   before this difficult time?

....

....

....

....

4. How did this difficult experience change your life?

....

....

....

....

5. What people played a key role during this time, whether
   good or bad?

....

....

....

....

Reminisce about a favorite car.

June 1963

My dad is kind of a "car guy." He loves cars! This '58 Chevrolet was his sixth car. He had four others and a pick-up truck. This one was his favorite. It was in mint condition and he took care of it really well - maintaining the engine and waxing the body. He sold it for $400 and says he still regrets it. He would love to have this beauty in his collection today!

Dwight and Ruthie

HIS favorite car

His Favorite Car BY VICKI HARVEY

Worksheet

A CAR STORY

1. Describe your first car (make, model, color, etc.).

_____

_____

_____

2. How did you raise the money or get the money to buy your car? How much did you pay for it?

_____

_____

_____

3. What did you love about your first car? What made you buy it?

_____

_____

_____

4. Describe some fond memories of your car (road trips, drive-in movies, etc.).

_____

_____

_____

5. Did you have any accidents in the car? Could the damage be repaired?

_____

_____

_____

Remember your best friends.

DELUXE CAN OPENERS
Safe to use! Smooth cut edges!
a modern kitchen appliance
3 Beautiful & easy to operate GREAT COLORS!

ZIPPY SIFTERS
Always start with
BEST for making your flour its FLUFFIEST for all your fine recipes.

Rose's stay fresh Cake Tins
FREE BONUS!
For cakes that stay fresh long after your party is over.

the **church basement ladies**

circa 1963

One of the most vivid childhood memories I have of my grandma is her working in the church kitchen with her friends. I could always find her stirring a pot or washing dishes at every bridal shower, anniversary celebration, wedding or funeral. In those days the church was the main place people socialized. You met friends there and breaking bread with them was a very important part of life. The ladies would gather in the kitchen and as they cooked and cleaned they would chat, gossip and generally solve the world's problems.

The Church Basement Ladies BY VICKI HARVEY

Worksheet

FRIENDSHIP

1. Tell about your best friend and how you got to know each other.

   _____

   _____

   _____

   _____

2. What characteristics do you admire about your best friend?

   _____

   _____

   _____

   _____

3. What other friends do you enjoy spending time with? What do you do together?

   _____

   _____

   _____

   _____

4. What disagreements have you had with a friend, and how were they resolved? Did they change your relationship?

   _____

   _____

   _____

   _____

5. How have your friends changed your life for the better?

   _____

   _____

   _____

   _____

A Lesson Learned

Living as a young adult during World War II was certainly an unforgettable experience for my Grandma. The many stories she shares with me are a window into both her and our country's past. While enduring those years as a young woman at war time, she definitely learned some life lessons that have stuck with her for the past 65 years. The army air raid warnings left a particular mark on her.

My Grandmother, Julie Rodriques, remembers the specific instructions they had to follow when the sirens went off in Santa Barbara, Ca. "Stop whatever you were doing. Turn off all the lights, no flashlights, no lighters, nothing. Close your painted black shades, take cover and wait."

She explains that it was a terrifying feeling for her and her brothers. "The sirens where very very loud." Her little brothers would ask "Is it real, sister? Are we going to die?" She would comfort them, as best she could, while dealing with her own fears.

This continued as she moved to San Diego in 1943 and became an aircraft riveter, building planes for the war. "It was worse there, the sirens went off more than ever". The lights would go out and they had to run to take cover under the huge, heavy work tables for aircraft construction. They would sometimes stay there 3 hours per night, until they would get the clear signal. She can still remember having to eat dinner in complete darkness.

"There was a lesson I learned through all of that" My Grandma tells me. "When you are a teen and a young adult, you don't necessarily like being ordered and bossed around. You think you know it all." But she wouldn't second guess the sirens and the instructions she had to follow. She knew it was for her safety and did them immediately. Through this, she learned to take directions and follow orders well; knowing many rules and ideas are there for our own good. From keeping a job, to keeping safe, she realized that following instruction and respecting the authority over us is key in life.

A Lesson Learned BY LEAH LaMONTAGNE

Worksheet

ALWAYS LEARNING

1. Out of all the lessons life has handed you, which one has been the most memorable? Why?

2. What did you learn from this experience?

3. How did it change your life?

4. How was this experience challenging or difficult for you?

5. What characteristic about yourself did you discover?

Journal about your spirituality.

Julie remembers her Grandmother, Minna Petersen, as a very spiritual person. They shared a special relationship, and Julie always felt so comfortable to speak with her about her faith.

While Julie was a young mother, Grandma Minna Petersen shared this precious story with her.

During the time when Minna was raising her six children in the 1930's, she became extremely sick. She was bedridden, unable to get up to take care of the family, or to work around the house. She described feeling miserable, without energy or hope for recovery. She felt desperation and was concerned that this may take her life. She worried about who would take care of the children.

Minna looked up, gazed out the window, and suddenly felt an incredible sense of God's comfort. In that moment, she knew He had heard her cries and understood her pain and anxiety. She felt His presence and knew He was there to help her. She was filled with hope.

Miraculously, only hours later, she was well and able to get out of bed and attend to her children and the home.

Minna held on to that experience and it seemed to give great inspiration to her Faith, as well as remind her that God was always with her. The story has also been a blessing to Julie, along with the other spiritual influences Grandma Petersen passed on to her.

Minna

Minna's story

Minna's Story BY LEAH LaMONTAGNE

Worksheet

SPIRITUALITY

1. What role has religion played in your life? Are you part of an organized religion? If so, why? If not, why?

   ....

   ....

   ....

   ....

2. What does spirituality mean to you?

   ....

   ....

   ....

   ....

3. How do you nurture your spiritual side?

   ....

   ....

   ....

   ....

4. What role does spirituality play in your everyday life?

   ....

   ....

   ....

   ....

5. How has your belief system been shaped by your spirituality (how you treat others, your belief in God, etc.)?

   ....

   ....

   ....

   ....

Page Planner 9

Use the page planner on the opposite page as a starting point for creating your own scrapbook pages. Here's how Carey used the page planner to tell a favorite family story.

Who doesn't love a parade? My grandparents, back in 1947, showed off their talents with this float for their business, Hartmann Studios. My grandmother sewed the costumes and helped to design the photos. I see that someone was able to get a quick photo of my grandpa jumping off the float. My grandma wrote on the back "the float in Arlington, 1947." My dad, Ron Hartmann, is the little camera man on the float.

I think he just looks so precious, and I wonder how in the world my grandparents got him to stick around enough to get these darling photos. He wasn't very old at the time. Maybe he was just a really good boy. What a clever couple of people they were.

PARADE

Parade BY CAREY JOHNSON

Tip: Create a simple, eye-catching design by journaling on colorful blocks. —*Carey Johnson*

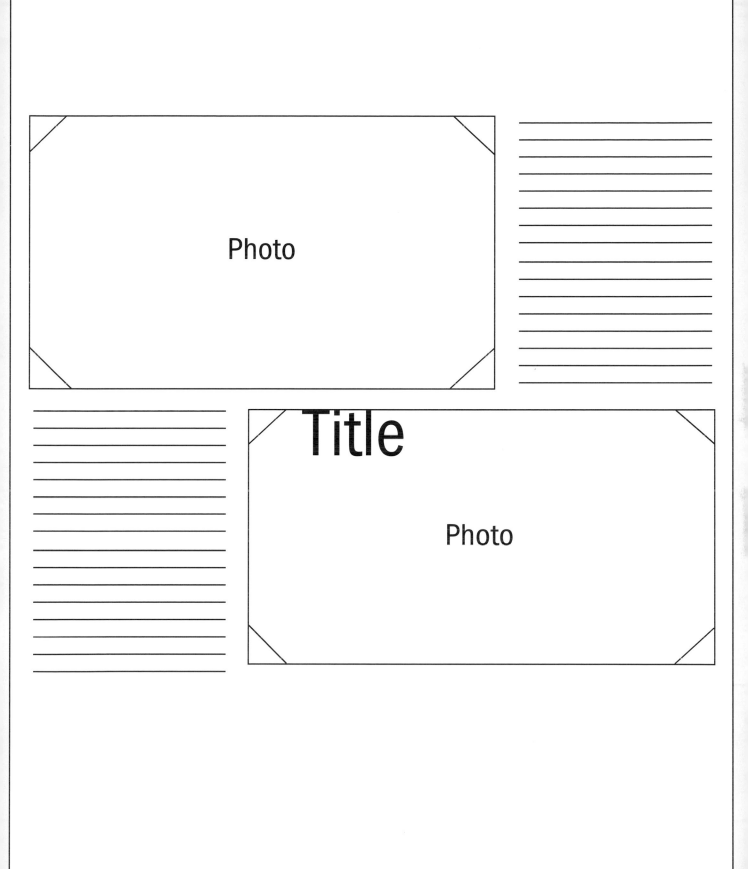

Page Planner 10

Use the page planner on the opposite page as a starting point for creating your own scrapbook pages. Here's how Carey used the page planner to tell a favorite family story.

Wanderlust BY CAREY JOHNSON

Tip: This layout shows that you can create a masculine heritage page and still use color! —*Carey Johnson*

Title

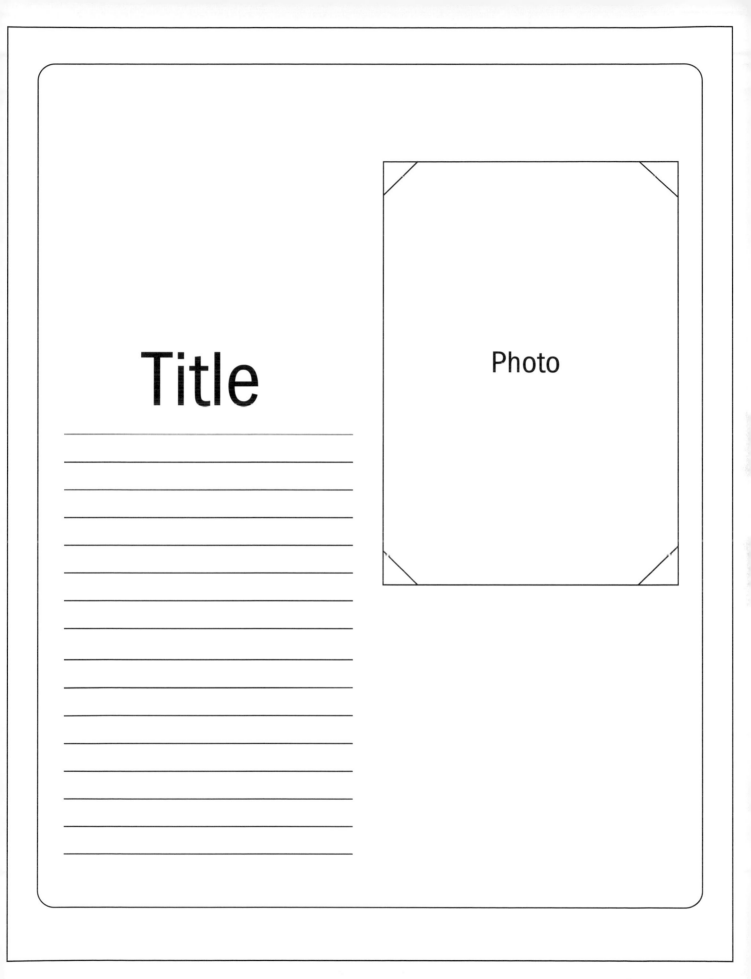

Photo

Family Album
Q&A with Leah LaMontagne

Diana's Childhood BY LEAH LaMONTAGNE

Why did you decide to create this album?

My husband's grandmother was happy when she learned I was interested in their family's history. She gave me a box full of her old photographs, knowing I would take care of them and appreciate them. I was so honored and excited to receive such a special gift. Since then, I've been calling her and discussing the memories and stories behind the photographs—pictures of her firstborn, who is my mother-in-law, were most prominent in the collection. I knew I had plenty of pictures and stories to easily fill a whole album. I thought they would be best preserved in a scrapbook of their own.

Why is this album important to you?

I want my children to know a lot about their family's past. When I was young, I enjoyed the occasional fun family story, but I wasn't that interested in pursuing an extensive knowledge of my family's past. I believe that family history scrapbooks, complete with pictures and interesting stories, will engage my kids' interest and ignite in them more interest in our heritage than I had as a little girl.

Is this a stand-alone album or part of a series?

It's a stand-alone album, although I plan to create separate albums for the other grandparents' and parents' childhood years.

How long did your project take?

I probably spent about two hours on each two-page layout. The album could probably be completed in 28 hours, including the album cover and contents page.

Childhood Favorites

Gail

Diana

Foods: Grandpa's deli sliced bologna & cheese, and Grandma's homemade pickles.
Treats: Black Licorice and ice cream.
Possessions: Dolls (they seemed so real) and my blue Schwinn bicycle.
Playmates: My younger brothers, and a friend down the street.
Games/Play: Hide and seek, Anti-Anti Over, Red Rover, throwing a ball over the house, climbing trees, and shooting beebee guns.
Holiday: Christmas. My Dad made it so magical, even if he didn't have the money.
Song: Jambalaya by Hank Williams Sr. I remember hearing that he was killed in the car accident in the early 50's and I asked my Mom if I would ever hear that song again. As kids did in those days, I thought he was in the Radio.
Book/Story: Three Little Pigs was the best, I also liked Red Riding Hood. At around 9 or 10, I liked the book Little Women.
School subject: Recess (loved the park) and Art.
Activities at home: To listen to radio shows & sing in the microphone to the record player.
Activities with Dad: Help him with projects, wash the car and shine the chrome, and jump in his pickup truck when he came home from work.
Activity with Mom: Sip a bottle of Coke with her in the afternoon, dry dishes, brush her hair and put bobby pins in it, and eat her baked treats while still warm from the oven.
Activities with Siblings: Watch their baseball games, play school, tea parties and dress up.
Color: Red. Especially red dresses.
Hobby: Making jewelry.
Animal: My dog. He'd wait at the corner when he knew I'd be coming home from school.
Article of clothing: The prettiest pair of pink silk Oriental Pajamas. They were from my Uncle Bob when he came home from the Korean War.
Winter activity: Eating snow Ice Cream (add milk, sugar & vanilla to snow), making snowmen, and to toboggan down the mountain.
Summer activity: Swimming! I lived for it. My Mom's Doctor had a swimming pool in his house. I used to draw pictures of it in art at school. I thought nothing could be better in life than having a swimming pool.
Gift received: For Christmas I wanted a black baby doll. I think it was made out of rubber. I just loved that doll, I can still remember the way it smelled.
Games: Monopoly, Old Maid, & Poker. (Grandma lived in Reno so we always had cards)
Thing that would get you in trouble: Being bossy with my brothers. It was my downfall.
Bible Story or Character: Noah, and the birth of Jesus.
Place in the house: From the upstairs bathroom we'd climb out onto the roof and sit there. I'm sure my Mom wasn't thrilled with that, but we couldn't resist.
Place in the yard: Up in the Lilac tree. The purple flowers smelled so good.

What's your best advice on family history scrapbooking?

If you have the desire to create a scrapbook about the life of a family member who is still living, don't wait! It's such a blessing and so much better to gather ideas and information from that person directly. Plus, he or she will be so honored and happy to know you're creating an entire scrapbook based on his or her life.

It can make anyone feel special when others take interest in their past, and dedicate their time and effort into preserving it. So, don't wait before it's too late to get all the stories and memories you can while they're still available, and while you still have the chance to make that someone feel so loved with a scrapbook dedicated to his or her life.

chapter 6

Family Traditions

"In each family a story is playing itself out, and each family's story embodies its hope and despair." — *Auguste Napier*

Reminisce about your family's favorite traditions.

Nativity STORY

1969 Nancy holding baby Joah, Sally, Jim, Tom, John & Rita holding Mary... Christmas time in Yakima, WA

1958 shepherds Tom, Sally & Jim...angel Nancy...John as Joseph... Rita as the blessed Mary...Mary as the infant Jesus

Your Grandma Nancy recalls acting out the nativity story at Christmas from as early as she can remember until the she and her siblings all got too old and then starting the tradition again with the next generation at Grandma Christine's house once there were enough grandkids to fill the roles. No one, though, can remember how the tradition began...perhaps thanks to the many costumes Grandma Christine would have made for the kids in their roles at St. Paul's school plays...perhaps just a whim. Grandma Christine says carrying the tradition over for the grandkids was meant to emphasize the meaning of Christmas, as they were all attending public schools and not receiving that instruction. I personally never witnessed this particular tradition but have heard many of the cousins discussing it with great fondness.

Nativity Story BY AMANDA PROBST

Worksheet

A HOLIDAY TRADITION

1. What is one of your favorite family traditions? Why?

....

....

....

....

2. How did this tradition come to be?

....

....

....

....

3. Are your extended family members involved in the tradition and in what capacity?

....

....

....

....

4. What other traditions do you enjoy?

....

....

....

....

5. How will you carry on the tradition?

....

....

....

....

I grew up in Prosser, WA…a little town of fewer than 5000 people located in the middle of nowhere (this was in 1993 when I left for college). At that time, the town didn't even have a single traffic light but was known for its high school sports programs and great schools. The motto (as stated on a huge traffic sign upon entering the town) was "Prosser: A Pleasant Place with Pleasant People." I heard that recently the motto has been changed, which leads me to wonder when and how the motto I know came to be.

Thanks to my Washington State history teacher, I know that Prosser became a town in 1899, having been a popular native American fishing area. Since its earliest days, though, Prosser has been an agricultural community, boasting many orchards, wheat farms and now wineries (and, at one point in the early 1900s as many as nine taverns).

It must have been the farming opportunities that drew my great-grandparents Anton & Antonia Smith and their kids to the area in 1918. The story goes that Antonia was looking to leave East Helena, MT where the rest of their friends and relatives were…wanting to get her sons away from the family tavern there. They'd set out, then, to settle in Pendleton, OR. On the train ride there, though, apparently Grandpa Anton got to talking with someone and was convinced that Prosser was the better route. Just like that, the family decided to settle in Prosser instead.

My Grandpa (Steve) Smith worked on some of the wheat farms up on Horse Heaven Hills and then purchased his own farm in 1936. He (with the help of his brother Jack) built a house and started a family two years later, bringing his wife home after marrying in East Helena. Grandpa Smith was an active member of the Prosser community, particularly involved in the Sacred Heart Catholic Church. (The gathering hall there is partially named for him, thanks to generous donations of time and money on his part.) He raised all eight of his children in Prosser and saw many of them return to raise their own families there. (Today, three of the eight continue to live in Prosser.)

A PLEASANT PLACE WITH PLEASANT PEOPLE

My dad (your Papa Robert) is a true Prosserite, having spent almost all his life there. He went to Prosser schools, left for college (staying in Washington still, though), took a teaching job in the Battlefield School District in Vancouver, WA where he taught 3rd grade for two years and then returned to Prosser to take up the family farm with his oldest brother, Steve. Since then, he and Steve have branched out from the family wheat farm to include also orchards, produce sales and viticulture. Steve remains on Horse Heaven on the family farm while my dad takes care of the orchards and wine grapes off the hill.

I, then, grew up on the family orchard just outside of Prosser. We had apples and cherries at the time and it's the only house I remember. (We moved there when I was about five and your Nana, Papa & Gramma Robbie still live there.) I loved growing up in a small town, where I knew most people and they knew me, particularly in school (where I even had some of the same teachers as my dad had) and at church. I sometimes miss that sense of community but have no plans at present to return to Prosser for more than visits. I'm sure it's changed since I left there. In my mind's eye, though, it will always be a pleasant place with pleasant people.

A Pleasant Place with Pleasant People BY AMANDA PROBST

Tip: I didn't have any photos for this layout, so I focused on the journaling instead, adding the title to break up a big block of text and colorizing the letters using markers. The subtle addition of color, I think, serves to keep the emphasis on the story. —*Amanda Probst*

Worksheet

OUR HOMETOWN

1. What is the name of your hometown? Describe some of the details.

_____

_____

_____

_____

2. If you were a tour guide in your hometown, where would you take visitors?

_____

_____

_____

_____

3. What are some of your favorite memories of your hometown?

_____

_____

_____

_____

4. If you still live in your hometown, how has it changed over the past five years?

_____

_____

_____

_____

5. If you moved a lot growing up, what do you consider your hometown?

_____

_____

_____

_____

Remember a special recipe.

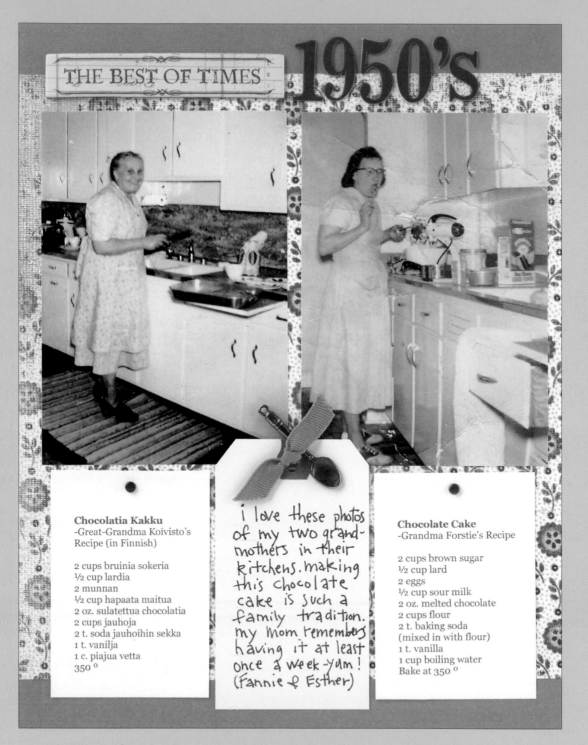

THE BEST OF TIMES

1950's

Chocolatia Kakku
-Great-Grandma Koivisto's
Recipe (in Finnish)

2 cups bruinia sokeria
½ cup lardia
2 munnan
½ cup hapaata maitua
2 oz. sulatettua chocolatia
2 cups jauhoja
2 t. soda jauhoihin sekka
1 t. vanilja
1 c. piajua vetta
350 °

i love these photos
of my two grand-
mothers in their
kitchens. making
this chocolate
cake is such a
family tradition.
my mom remembers
having it at least
once a week - yum!
(Fannie & Esther)

Chocolate Cake
-Grandma Forstie's Recipe

2 cups brown sugar
½ cup lard
2 eggs
½ cup sour milk
2 oz. melted chocolate
2 cups flour
2 t. baking soda
(mixed in with flour)
1 t. vanilla
1 cup boiling water
Bake at 350 °

The Best of Times BY KIM KESTI

Tip: I wanted to include two recipes on this layout so I printed them on the computer to make them easier to fit on the layout. To add a personal touch, I added a handwritten note. Even though the quality of these photos isn't the best, I just love the personality that shines through. —*Kim Kesti*

Worksheet

FAMILY RECIPES

1. My favorite recipe for _____ from _____ .

   Memories: _____

   _____

   Recipe: _____

   _____

   _____

   _____

2. My favorite recipe for _____ from _____ .

   Memories: _____

   _____

   Recipe: _____

   _____

   _____

   _____

3. My favorite recipe for _____ from _____ .

   Memories: _____

   _____

   Recipe: _____

   _____

   _____

   _____

4. My favorite recipe for _____ from _____ .

   Memories: _____

   _____

   Recipe: _____

   _____

   _____

   _____

Journal about your family values.

Pray

Faith has always been an important part of our family life. All the way back to when our ancestors immigrated to Northen Minnesota and Michigan, they hosted church services in their homes until the community could afford to build a church. The church pictured here was one built on land donated by Matt and Maria Koivisto in Finlayson, Minnesota. It was built around 1900.

Work

A good honest day's work has always had value in our family. Our Forstie ancestors ran a successful farm including a dairy that served the local community. The Dairy operated until pasteurized milk became common. Grandpa Art was the youngest of 14 children and knew what it was to work. Only Sunday was set aside for worship and relaxation.

Play

Summer was fleeting in Northern Minnesota and money was short, so families headed often to the local rivers and lakes. This photo was taken at Round Lake, Minnesota where the Forstie family enjoyed many picnics and family gatherings. A good balance of work and play grew strong families back in the 1940's.

Our Family Values BY KIM KESTI

Worksheet

OUR VALUES

1. What family values did you learn from your parents?

_____

_____

_____

2. What values do you want to pass on to your children? Why?

_____

_____

_____

3. What one value do you feel is the most important to possess?

_____

_____

_____

4. Tell about an incident growing up in which you were taught an important lesson about a specific value.

_____

_____

_____

5. What value do you think today's generation is lacking?

_____

_____

_____

Laugh about a funny family story.

happy

IF YOU EVER DARED TO TELL IRENE ABERCROMBIE YOU WERE BORED YOU'D ALWAYS GET THE SAME REPLY: GO OUT-SIDE — FIND SOMETHING TO MAKE YOUR SELF HAPPY. ON THIS DAY BACK IN '61 LORI AND LEDA DID JUST THAT. THEY AMUSED THE WHOLE FAMILY (AND NEIGHBORHOOD!) WITH THEIR IMPROMPTU HOBO ACT. THEY HAD EVERYONE IN STITCHES OVER THEIR FUNNY SONG + DANCE.

Happy BY SHELLEY LAMING

Worksheet

A FUNNY STORY

1. Tell about a funny family story.

   ....
   ....
   ....
   ....

2. Why was this incident so comical?

   ....
   ....
   ....

3. What individuals were involved in the funny incident?

   ....
   ....
   ....

4. What things remind you of this story?

   ....
   ....
   ....

5. Did you feel bad for anyone involved in the story? If so, why?

   ....
   ....
   ....

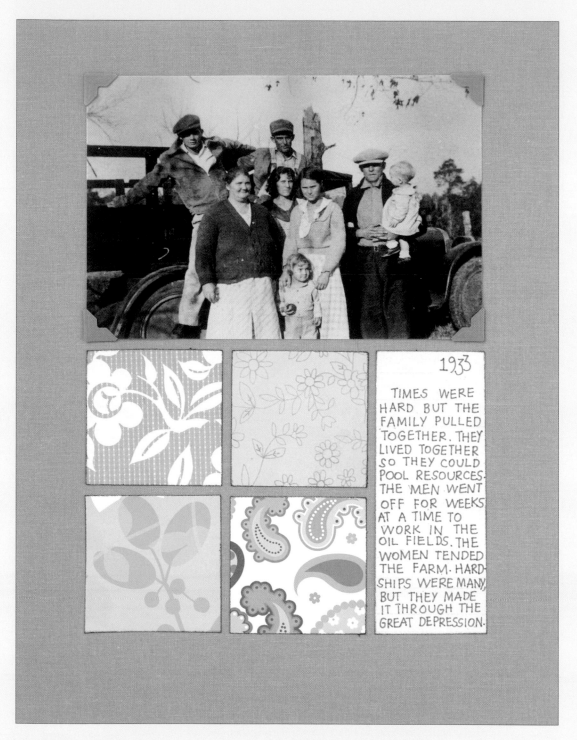

1933 BY SHELLEY LAMING

1933

TIMES WERE HARD BUT THE FAMILY PULLED TOGETHER. THEY LIVED TOGETHER SO THEY COULD POOL RESOURCES. THE MEN WENT OFF FOR WEEKS AT A TIME TO WORK IN THE OIL FIELDS. THE WOMEN TENDED THE FARM. HARDSHIPS WERE MANY, BUT THEY MADE IT THROUGH THE GREAT DEPRESSION.

Worksheet

A SERIOUS STORY

1. Talk about a serious family story.

_____

_____

_____

_____

2. How did you feel about what happened?

_____

_____

_____

_____

3. Who was involved, and how did it impact them?

_____

_____

_____

_____

4. Does it still impact your family today? How?

_____

_____

_____

_____

5. What did you learn from this event?

_____

_____

_____

_____

Reminisce about a family heirloom.

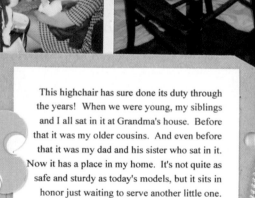

through the
years

This highchair has sure done its duty through the years! When we were young, my siblings and I all sat in it at Grandma's house. Before that it was my older cousins. And even before that it was my dad and his sister who sat in it. Now it has a place in my home. It's not quite as safe and sturdy as today's models, but it sits in honor just waiting to serve another little one.

Christmas 1968

Through the Years BY VICKI HARVEY

Worksheet

A FAMILY HEIRLOOM

1. Describe a family heirloom.

   ....

   ....

   ....

   ....

2. Who originally acquired the piece? How did he or she get it, and why did he or she keep it?

   ....

   ....

   ....

   ....

3. Who has the heirloom now and how was it passed down?

   ....

   ....

   ....

   ....

4. What fond memories do you have of the family heirloom?

   ....

   ....

   ....

   ....

5. Did your family come close to losing the heirloom, or was it ever in danger of being destroyed? Describe what happened.

   ....

   ....

   ....

   ....

Share the meaning behind family jewelry.

GRANDMA'S locket

When my grandmother Lucile passed away I inherited her beautiful engraved locket. I was so thrilled to find this family photo with her actually wearing the locket. She was about seven years old in this photo. She is with her parents Minnie and Lewis Trumbull and her baby brother Lelynn.

Circa 1911

199728

Grandma's Locket BY VICKI HARVEY

Tip: I printed my journaling on cardstock and then hand-cut it into a tag shape. I added a punched circle for the reinforcement on the top. —*Vicki Harvey*

Worksheet

A FAMILY JEWEL

For each piece of jewelry, answer the following questions. Feel free to include a photo as well!

1. What is it:_____
   First acquired by_____ at this price:_____
   The significance of the piece:_____
   Where it is now:_____
   A memory I have of the piece:_____

   _____

   _____

2. What is it:_____
   First acquired by_____ at this price:_____
   The significance of the piece:_____
   Where it is now:_____
   A memory I have of the piece:_____

   _____

   _____

3. What is it:_____
   First acquired by_____ at this price:_____
   The significance of the piece:_____
   Where it is now:_____
   A memory I have of the piece:_____

   _____

   _____

4. What is it:_____
   First acquired by_____ at this price:_____
   The significance of the piece:_____
   Where it is now:_____
   A memory I have of the piece:_____

   _____

   _____

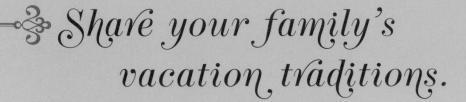

Share your family's vacation traditions.

Green Valley Lake
California

With three young daughters, Dick & Millie Petersen took several spring and summer visits to Green Valley Lake, Ca. Millie's parents, Harold & Hildegarde, along with her Sister and Brother-in-law, bought a fixer-upper cabin there in the 1950's. In his retirement years, Harold put his carpenter expertise to work and repaired and remodeled it into a charming getaway. The mountainous lake surroundings of tall pine trees and winding roads made a relaxing atmosphere for the family to spend time together. At the lake, they enjoyed swimming, boating, or walking with the little girls, Julie, Debbie, and Laurie. Harold & Hildegarde loved having their granddaughters visit, and always made the family feel so welcomed.

Green Valley Lake BY LEAH LaMONTAGNE

Worksheet

VACATION TRADITIONS

1. Describe the details of a favorite family trip.

_____

_____

_____

2. What made this particular trip so much fun?

_____

_____

_____

3. What regular annual trips did your family take? What is your favorite memory of these trips?

_____

_____

_____

4. What modes of transportation did your family use to travel? (What were road trips like for your family? What would you do to pass the time? Did you travel by car, train or airplane?)

_____

_____

_____

5. What individuals, including extended family, were involved in family trips?

_____

_____

_____

Record your family's favorite sayings.

If He Said it Once, He'll Say it Again.

Dick Petersen is known in the Family as always having a quotable phrase for any situation. Through the years, he's collected countless expressions and has introduced them into the lives of each succeeding generation. They've become so familiar, that we find ourselves reciting them too; and if we are quick enough, we can even beat him to the punch when we sense that he is about to say one!

Here is a sampling of the Family's most memorable Dick sayings:

Up & Adam
It's not worth the paper it's written on
Clean your room. (kids: We did Dad.) Do it again!
Don't let the door hit you in the rear on the way out
He has a good head on his shoulders
Good gravy!
Good night!
Don't be a cry baby
Put some elbow grease into it
Blind as a bat
Keep your mitts off!
Don't put all your eggs in one basket
He's trying to pull a fast one
Don't cry over spilled milk
The higher you climb the harder the fall
Stubborn as a mule
A bird in the hand is worth 2 in the bush
I'm glad you got to talk to me
Dog-gone-it!
Now were moving on an even keel
Deader than a doornail
You make a better door than a window
Only once in a blue moon
I'm gonna go hit the sack
Pain in the neck
From here to kingdom come
Don't blow your top
That burns me up!
If you believe that, I've got a bridge I could sell you
You've heard my side of the story, now don't bother me with yours
Remove the boulder in your own eye before seeing the speck in your neighbor's

If He Said It Once . . . BY LEAH LaMONTAGNE

Tip: When gathering family quotes, get the whole family involved. You'll get even more information—and have more fun! —*Leah LaMontagne*

Worksheet

FAVORITE FAMILY SAYINGS

1. Does your family have a favorite saying? What is it?

   ....

   ....

   ....

2. How did this saying come to be?

   ....

   ....

   ....

3. Does your family use special signals to communicate with each other when other people are around?

   ....

   ....

   ....

4. What people outside of your family have picked up a phrase coined by your family?

   ....

   ....

   ....

5. What other sayings does your family use?

   ....

   ....

   ....

Use the page planner on the opposite page as a starting point for creating your own scrapbook pages. Here's how Carey used the page planner to tell a favorite family story.

For Barb's 60th Birthday, she wanted to recreate this photo. The top photo is of Bob's grandma in the buggy and his great-great grandmother with her grandchildren at Sibley Park in Mankato, MN. It was taken sometime around 1918. I took this photo of my mother-in-law 88 years later on the day of her 60th birthday, August 6th, 2006. It was taken in front of the very same fountain. Pretty cool!

Then Grandmas & Now Grandchildren Parks & Play

Then & Now BY CAREY JOHNSON

Tip: Don't be afraid to mix old and new photographs on your page. —*Carey Johnson*

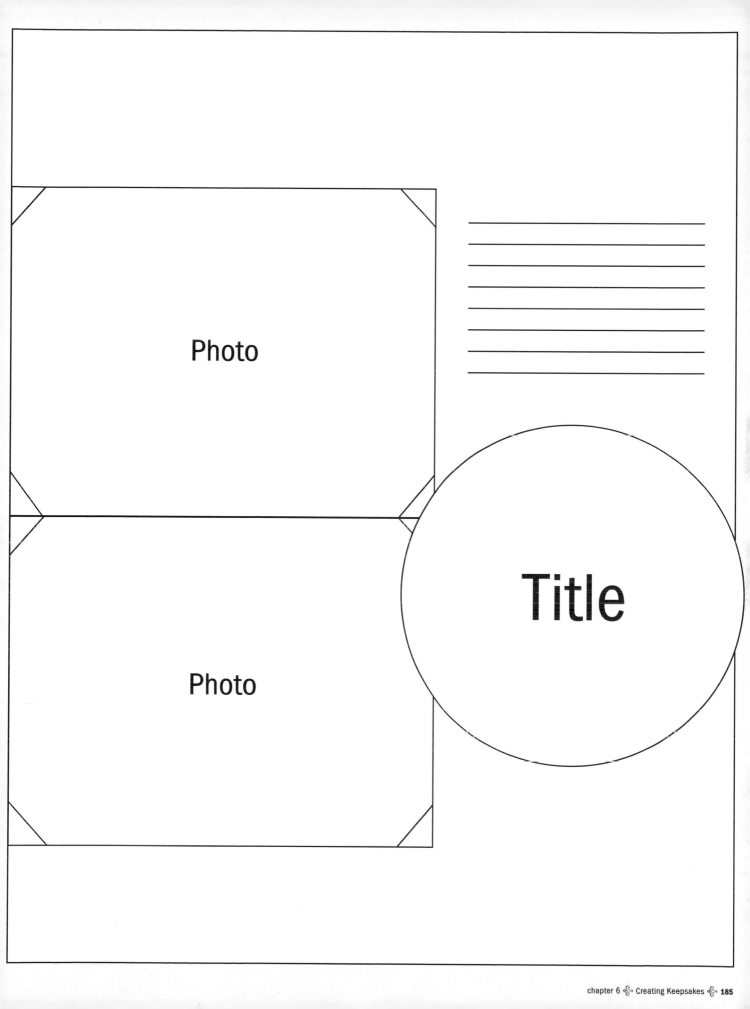

Photo

Photo

Title

Use the page planner on the opposite page as a starting point for creating your own scrapbook pages. Here's how Carey used the page planner to tell a favorite family story.

Four weeks on the road...six people in a car; no leg room because the tent was on the floor ...but, my dad says that on his trip toCalifornia, they saw Yosemite, Yellowstone, The Grand Canyon, learned to body surf, visited his uncle's ship and much much more. I think the tradition of a family trip, not vacation ...we Hartmanns don't seem to DO vacations ...we go on trips, started way back in 1958 with this trip.

Travel BY CAREY JOHNSON

Tip: This is a great way to use those little square photos from the 1940s and 50s. —*Carey Johnson*

Title

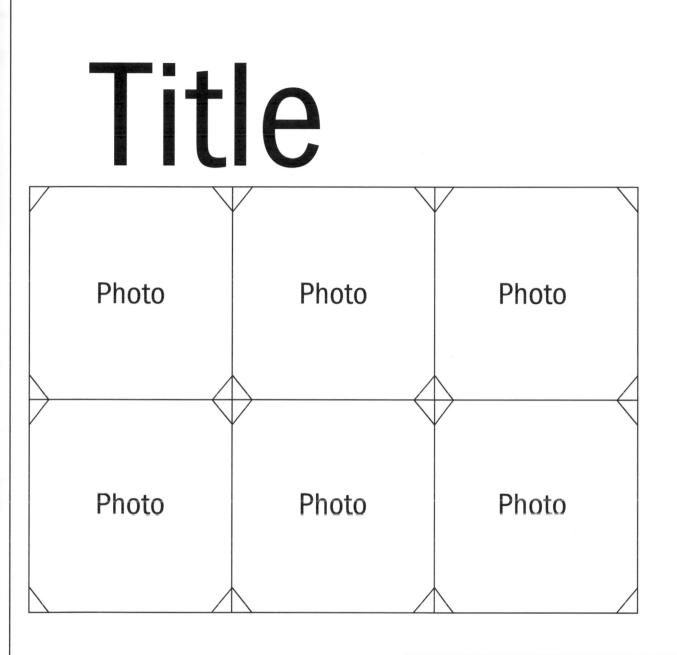

Childhood: My Favorite Images of My
Favorite People as Children BY CAREY JOHNSON

Why did you decide to create this album?

I love literature, poetry and music, and I thought this would be a great way
to incorporate my love of poetry within the mosaic of the life of my kin. I
can focus on favorite photos and topics while incorporating poetry.

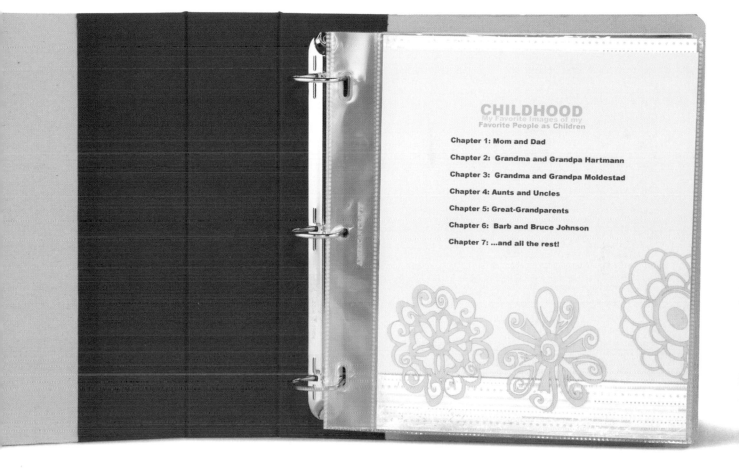

CHILDHOOD
My Favorite Images of my
Favorite People as Children

Chapter 1: Mom and Dad

Chapter 2: Grandma and Grandpa Hartmann

Chapter 3: Grandma and Grandpa Moldestad

Chapter 4: Aunts and Uncles

Chapter 5: Great-Grandparents

Chapter 6: Barb and Bruce Johnson

Chapter 7: ...and all the rest!

Why is this album important to you?

Well, heritage is important to me, so I'm all for any way I can display my heritage while showcasing my grandpa's photography.

Is this a stand-alone album or part of a series?

This is one of many heritage albums, but I created only one dedicated to this theme.

Birthdays WERE **HUGE** H artmann in the OUSEHOLD

There are so many photos of my dad and his siblings on their birthdays. This photo was taken on my Dad's second birthday. My grandma seemed to always make a great cake and there are usually friends and relatives in all of the pictures.

RONALD HARTMANN

(2)

How long did your project take?

It took me about 16 hours to complete.

The Calm Before the Storm I don't have a lot of photos of my mom when she was a child, but this is one of my favorites for a few reasons. I think she looks adorable. I love the smile on my grandpa's face; he looks so proud and happy! I am wondering what exactly my grandma's coat was made out of, and I know that around this time my grandma must have been pregnant with my aunt and uncle...and then, I know life would never be this quiet or this simple for my mom again. She was a big sister!

What's your best advice on family history scrapbooking?

Use the computer as much as possible. Collect favorite poems and songs and keep them in a file. Find photos that represent some of these favorite items and merge the two together. Tie yourself to your own heritage. When you're looking at the photos in your pile and are getting ready to start scrapbooking, ask yourself what you already know about the topic and list those items in one column on a piece of paper. Then in another column, write what you want or need to know before you start. This really helped me figure out questions I needed to ask my dad or other family members before I tried to journal or figure out the mood of the photos.

Index

Bonus

See page 11 to learn how to download all of the checklists, forms, page planners and worksheets in this book for *FREE*.

Supplies